YOU CAN U with beakman & jax

More Science Stuff You Can Do

by JOK CHURCH

Andrews and McMeel

A Universal Press Syndicate Company

Kansas City

Library of Congress Cataloging-in-Publication Data

Church, Jok.
    You can with Beakman & Jax : more science
stuff you can do / by Jok Church.
            p.   cm.
        ISBN: 0-8362-7008-8 : $8.95
        1. Science Experiments—Juvenile literature. 2.
Science-
-Miscellanea—Juvenile literature. 3. Science—Comic
books, strips,
etc. Juvenile literature. [1. Science—Experiments.
2. Experiments. 3. Science—Miscellanea.] I. Title. II.
Title:
You can with Beakman & Jax.
Q164.C446   1994
94-7025
                                                507.8—dc20
                                                CIP
                                                AC

NOTE TO PARENTS:

You Can with Beakman & Jax: More Science Stuff You Can *Do* is intended to be educational and informative. It contains relatively simple science experiments designed to interest children. Many of the experiments require adult supervision. We strongly recommend that before you allow children to conduct any of the experiments in this book that you read the experiment in its entirety and make your own determination as to the safest way of conducting the experiment.

CONTENTS

Stuff *You Can* Do to Figure Out . . .

ABCs 7	Knuckle Cracks 82
Acid Rain 10	Lasers..................................85
Band-Aids™ 13	Leaf Colors.........................88
Bone Cracks 16	Levers 91
Bouncing 19	Locks...................................94
Bubbles..............................22	Lotion 97
Butterfly Wings 25	Melting Snow 100
Christmas Tree Lights 28	Mirrors 103
Daylight-saving Time......31	Newspaper Photos 106
Density 34	Night Sounds 109
Dust 37	Nuclear Energy 112
Eyeglasses 40	Paper Making 115
Feathers 43	Plastic...............................118
Fire Colors 46	Rock 'n' Roll 121
Fossils 49	Seedless Grapes 124
Fuzzy TVs..........................52	Sewage 127
Ghosts.................................55	Spider Webs.....................130
Glue 58	Strength 133
Goose Bumps 61	Taffy 136
Green Grass 64	Tires 139
Hair.....................................67	Toilets 142
Heart...................................70	Tooth Cavities.................145
Honey 73	Toys...................................148
Horoscopes 76	Vomit 151
Knives.................................79	Zippers 154

Greetings:

You Can with Beakman & Jax is the only newspaper comic strip drawn and colored on a computer. I use Adobe Systems programs like Illustrator and PhotoStop and want to say so even though they don't pay for this plug.

The patient and gifted graphics department at Universal Press Syndicate/Andrews and McMeel has transformed my comic's computer files into this book, a process that pushes hard at the boundaries of graphic arts. I am grateful to and honored to be associated with Julie Phillips and Susan Patton.

Deciding the differences between a comic strip and a book is this book's editor Dorothy O'Brien. It is she, with the assistance of Regan Brown, who created continuity in this book.

Before I see the mail, the staff of UniMedia has opened and responded to the hundreds and hundreds of letters that Beakman and Jax receive. My thanks to Jeanne Oliver, Kathy Douglas, Nancy Meis, and Tom Stites.

I am indebted to the editorial staff of Universal Press Syndicate. My editor Lisa Tarry is aided by Alan McDermott, Barb Thompson, Joyce Mott, and Lee Salem. I honor and respect the work of Mr. Bob Duffy and his pack of warriors. Thanks also to Elena Fallon, Bev Shiels, Rita Denton, Jean Spreen, and David Sheffield. The support of Kathleen Andrews and John McMeel is also very important to me.

At-home love and enthusiasm comes from a community of friends led by Adam Cieselski, and which includes Robert Boccabella, Chloe Atkins, Hal Pierson, Glenn Peck, Marsha Fine, Von Wall, Mark Vincent, Kadi Kiiss, Tom Scott, Mike Thomas, Jim and Jan Church, Roy and Evelyn Hoffman, Earl and Flo Mills, Howard Roffman, Charles and Betty Church, Edgar Carpenter, Viola Weinberg, Jay Dubin, Mark Ritts, and Paul Zaloom.

Thanks also to the many people who have sent e-mail to *jok@nbn.com* and to the generous proprietor of the North Bay Network, John Harkin, for allowing me access to the Internet.

I know that you may have your own question. If so, please take your family to your local library and answer it. Coming up with the question is the hard part and you've already done that. Getting the answer is as simple as asking a librarian to show you how to find out. It feels good and is a good thing for families to do together. I do it every week at the San Rafael Public Library.

A percentage of the royalties of this book are donated to the Marin Food Bank because they feed kids.

A good question is a very powerful thing.
Keep answering them.

—Jok

For Susanne and Zoë . . .
. . . a blink ago babies,
now mothers themselves.

Dear Reader:

⚠ Please look for this special caution sign throughout this book. When you see this sign, it means that you need to ask a grown-up for help.

This is a book for families to use together so the grown-ups in your family should be happy to work with you.

Show your family this page.

Remember, look for this sign. It is very important. ⚠

Beakman

Beakman

Jax Place

Jax Place

Dear Jax,

Who came up with the ABCs?

Angela Bania
Chicago, Illinois

Dear Angela,

Alphabets are like computers. Computers store information, sort information and allow us to get it back – or retrieve it. That's what alphabets do, too.

You Can store, sort and retrieve any idea, any piece of information, any opinion with just 26 letters and 10 numerals. That's pretty amazing if you think about it. The alphabet we use is only one of many ways of writing in use today.

No one person invented our alphabet. Alphabets grew over thousands of years.

Jax Place

Jax Place

How Alphabets Began

History is the stuff that's written down. If it's before writing was invented, it's prehistoric – or before history.

The beginnings of our alphabet are prehistoric. The first alphabets *began history*.

Our alphabet started more than 5,000 years ago in the Middle East. People stopped using pictures just for decoration and began using them to record facts and ideas. The people who started this are called Proto-Semites.

A picture of an ox could mean ox. You'd need a picture for every word.

An easier way to draw an ox. By now it may have meant a sound.

Straight lines made it still easier. You could draw it with a brush or in wet clay.

People called the Phoenicians tipped it over. We don't really know why.

The ancient Greeks drew it like this. It was easy to carve in stone.

The Romans took lots of stuff from the Greeks. They gave the letter A the shape we use.

P.S. from Beakman: The word *alphabet* means the letters A and B. Alpha is the name of the letter A in Greek. Beta is the name of the letter B.

8

Create a New Alphabet

WHAT YOU NEED: Pencil - paper - your imagination

WHAT TO DO: Think of the sounds the letters of the alphabet make. These pictures are for **A**, **B** and **C** – Apple, Bat and Car. Draw pictures for the letters that spell your name.

Next, make the drawings very simple. Think about having to draw them over and over again quickly. What would the pictures turn into?

Now *forget* about what they are pictures of. Just look at the shapes and make them even more simple. It can still mean ABC, but now it's a completely new alphabet. Make A through Z with your friends. You'll have a secret code for notes and letters no one else can read.

Dear Beakman,

How can rain be acid rain?

Carolynne Good
Stratford,
Ontario

Dear Carolynne,

That's a question more and more Canadians are asking the United States. More and more rain in Eastern Canada is acidic. Air pollution in the United States seems to be the reason why.

It's happening in the U.S.A., too. Rain as acidic as lemon juice fell in Wheeling, West Virginia, and many lakes in New York State are dying from acid rain. Also there's acid rain in Germany's Black Forest.

Acid rain starts out as regular rain. But when it falls through clouds of air pollution, rain changes into a weak acid. This acid is strong enough to kill trees, dissolve marble and kill whole lakes.

Beakman
Beakman Place

Make an Acid Tester

WHAT YOU NEED:

Red cabbage - saucepan - grater - water - help and permission from an adult

WHAT TO DO: Finely grate the red cabbage till you have 2 cups. Just cover with water and bring to a boil. Do not use an aluminum pan! ⚠ *Never use the stove without permission from your family.* Simmer for 15 minutes. Let it cool, then strain and save the liquid.

WHAT IS GOING ON: I know it's like cabbage tea and that seems a bit disgusting. But cabbage tea is also an *indicator*. That means if you add acid to your acid tester, it will change color. Test different things. Add 1 teaspoon of vinegar to 1 teaspoon of cabbage tea. What happens? It changes color to light pink. Do the same test with a pinch of baking soda, and the juice turns blue. Do your tests in a small clear glass so you can hold it up to light.

Your acid tester will change from pink for acids to green for alkalines (AL-ka-linz) – which is the opposite of acids. Things that aren't acid or alkaline are called neutral (NEW-trahl) and are right in the middle.

Testing Rainwater

WHAT YOU NEED: Your acid tester cabbage tea

WHAT TO DO: Test other things with your acid tester, like soap or lemon juice. You'll see what's acidic and what's alkaline. Now start collecting rainwater samples in very clean jars that you've rinsed out extra especially well. Label and date the jars.

Mix equal amounts of your acid tester with your samples of rainwater. Make notes on any color changes. It should stay the same. If the color starts moving to the reds and pinks, you may be getting acid rain.

pinks	reds	purple	blues	greens
Acid		Neutral		Alkaline

Take your rain samples to school. Your teacher can use another acid tester that's more accurate. It's called litmus paper. If your class finds any acid rain, you might want to write a class letter to your representative in Congress or Parliament.

P.S. from Jax: Acid rain is not new. It was first discovered in England in 1872. Smoke from coal was the cause. Coal and oil smoke are still the problem, 120 years later.

Dear Beakman,

How does a Band-Aid™ stop bleeding?

Sheila Novelli
West Falls,
New York

Dear Sheila,

Band-Aid™ is a brand name. That means a company actually owns that word. But I think you're really asking about all stick-on bandages. And they do not stop bleeding.

Blood is better on the inside. So your body makes a kind of bandage for itself that stops blood from leaking out.

The stick-on bandages lots of people like have a different job. They keep a wound clean.

The bandage your body makes is called a scab.

Beakman

Beakman Place

Blood -
Not Really Red

Blood is not really a thick, red liquid. Instead, it's a clear liquid with lots of little stuff floating in it. That little stuff is mostly red blood cells, which is why blood looks red. Flowing through the tiny veins in our bodies, the cells line up like in this drawing. The little bits floating with the cells are very important when it comes to stopping leaks. They are called platelets.

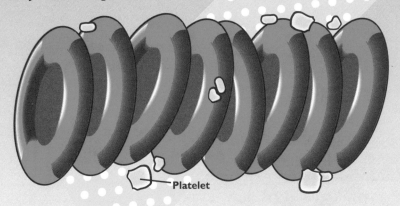

Platelet

When a vein gets torn open, blood starts leaking. The platelets are there to stop the leak. They flow to the tear and start patching it up. Platelets then send out a complicated chemical signal that tells our body to start making a chemical called fibrin (FI-bren). Fibrin is like tiny threads that flow to the tear and build a net that traps the blood cells and keeps them from leaking out. When this happens on our skin, we call it a scab. A scab plugs the leak. Under it, our skin cells repair themselves.

When You Do Get Hurt

When we get hurt and bleed, lots of times we're really scared. That fear may make the hurt seem bigger than it is. Sometimes when we stick a bandage on a little hurt, it can make us feel better just because we know that someone is taking care of us – usually someone in our family.

The bandage can keep the cut clean, which is very important to healing. But it also can just make us *feel better* about getting hurt. And that's OK.

Remember, the scab is the real plug that stops the bleeding, so don't pick it off. It will wear off by itself as you heal.

Take a Closer Look

Blood and bleeding are very serious stuff. It's impossible for Jax and me to tell you everything you need to know about a big subject like first aid.

But, it's pretty easy to find all the information you need. 4-H, Boy Scouts, Girl Scouts, Camp Fire, the Y, J.C.C. and The Red Cross all have courses and books on first aid. There are also books on it in your school library.

P.S. from Jax: There doesn't seem to be any way to take off a stick-on bandage that doesn't hurt. Most everyone hates that. What really hurts is the sticky stuff grabbing little hairs on our skin and yanking them out.

Dear Beakman,

Sometimes my feet crack when I walk. Why?

Brandon Clifton
Hudsonville,
Michigan

Dear Brandon,

Our bones are the things that keep us from being big blobs. Our bones hold us up. When we move our bones, sometimes there are sounds. There are *snaps* and there are *cracks*.

Neither one of those sounds comes from our bones at all. The sounds come from the muscles and tendons that hold our bones together.

Your feet and ankles aren't really cracking. *You Can* build a simple model of a joint to understand.

Beakman

Beakman Place

My Dinner with Anatomy

WHAT YOU NEED: Talk to whomever cooks in your family. Ask for a roasted chicken for dinner – a whole chicken. Tell them it's for science and be polite. That should work. It usually does.

WHAT TO DO: Save the leg bones (drumsticks) and the thigh bones. Fit them together and pretend they're still connected. Bend them back and forth. Take a close look. See how things work. Someone might say you're playing with your food. Tell them you're making an examination.

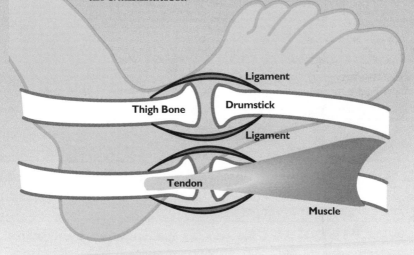

Ligament

Thigh Bone Drumstick

Ligament

Tendon

Muscle

WHAT IS GOING ON: *You Can* see that without the meat, bones don't hold together at all. There are two things that hold bones together – ligaments (LIG-ah-mentz) and tendons (TEN-dunz).

Ligaments connect bone to bone. Tendons connect muscles to bones. Both jump across the joint and hold the bones together.

And both can pop and snap when your muscles move your bones. That's what makes the *crack* in your feet.

17

Make a Joint

WHAT YOU NEED: Toilet paper roll - scissors - wide rubber band - stapler

WHAT TO DO: Cut the tube in the middle, but not all the way around. Bend it down like a hinge. Now straighten it out. Cut the rubber band and *stretch* it along the top of the tube across the cut. Staple it at both ends of the tube.

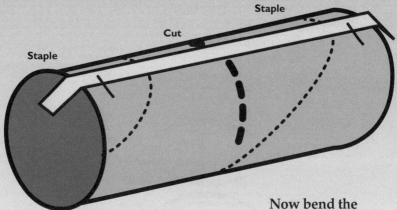

Staple

Cut

Staple

Now bend the tube down on the hinge you made. Sometimes the rubber band will stay on the top of the tube. Sometimes it pops off.

WHAT IS GOING ON: Muscles and tendons slip and snap just like your rubber band, only not as much. It's a lot of noise for such a little thing, but think how much sound you can make snapping chewing gum.

P.S. from Jax: When your knuckles crack, the sound is made in a different way. Very different. See page 82 to find out how different.

Dear Jax,

Why does a rubber ball bounce?

Tianna Nelson
Castro Valley,
California

Dear Tianna,

When you drop a ball and the ball falls to the ground, the energy of the fall actually collapses the bottom of the ball.

When the ball reshapes itself, that falling energy is changed into lifting energy.

After you do this experiment, *You Can* read the reason it works by holding page 21 up to a mirror.

Jax Place
Jax Place

The Way the Ball Bounces

WHAT YOU NEED: Basketball - tennis ball
*Optional: Any other 2 balls that are about the same sizes –
1 very big and 1 quite small. They both should bounce.*

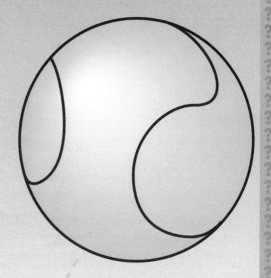

WHAT TO DO: Put a ball in each of your hands. Gently turn your hands over at the same time. Let the balls fall to the ground. Do not add any energy by pushing or throwing them down.

MORE STUFF TO DO: Now place the tennis ball on top of the basketball. Let them drop together. Again, do not add any energy by throwing the balls down to the ground.

SO WHAT: The balls bounced at about the same height during the first part of your experiment. But when you did the second part, the tennis ball zoomed off and jumped as high as a house. Why?

20

What Is Going On

When you bounced the balls separately, they both popped back up about the same height. And that's important if you think about it. The basketball is much bigger and is a lot heavier than the tennis ball. That means a lot more energy is needed to lift that ball up in its bounce. The tennis ball takes less energy to lift in its bounce. When you put the two together, some of the lifting energy is transferred from the basketball to the tennis ball. It was so much, the tennis ball shot off like a rocket.

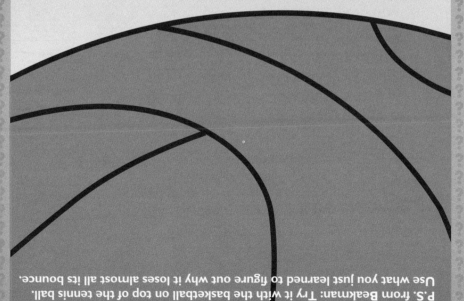

P.S. from Beakman: Try it with the basketball on top of the tennis ball. Use what you just learned to figure out why it loses almost all its bounce.

Dear Beakman,

Can you make square bubbles?

Jennifer West
Winnipeg,
Manitoba

Dear Jennifer,

Yes, *You Can* make a square bubble. But you have to force it.

Bubbles can teach you a lot about chemistry and geometry. Also, blowing weirdly shaped and extra-large bubbles is a lot of fun.

The bubble formula I have for you might upset 2 groups of people – the folks who sell it in those teeny tiny bottles, and your family, because of the mess.

Take the mess and the fun outside into the sun.

Beakman

Beakman Place

Beakman's Bubbles

Better and Lots Cheaper

WHAT YOU NEED: Liquid dishwashing soap - glycerine (from drugstore) - gallon jug - dishpan or other large flat pan, like a big cake pan

WHAT TO DO: Add $2/3$ cup of the soap to a gallon of water. Add the soap last so you don't get a jug full of suds. Add 1 tablespoon of glycerine, which will help your bubbles last longer. Ask the people at the drugstore for it. You may want to experiment by trying things like Jell-O, Certo or even sugar instead. I use glycerine.

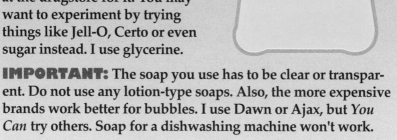

IMPORTANT: The soap you use has to be clear or transparent. Do not use any lotion-type soaps. Also, the more expensive brands work better for bubbles. I use Dawn or Ajax, but *You Can* try others. Soap for a dishwashing machine won't work.

MORE STUFF TO DO: Stir it well and let the formula sit for a while. Pour several inches of it into your pan. When using the bubble tools you're going to make, make sure your hands are really wet with the formula. Ditto for the bubble tools. Bubbles break when something dry touches them – even a piece of dust. The way you think and behave is important, too. Be gentle and slow while learning to work with your tools. Then it's O.K. to get crazy and radical. If it's windy outside, come inside and work at the sink.

Bubble Stuff

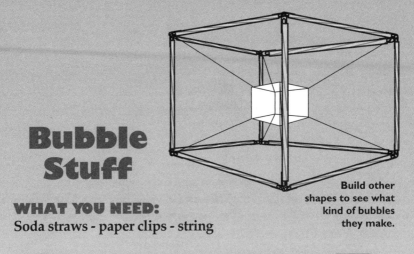

Build other shapes to see what kind of bubbles they make.

WHAT YOU NEED:
Soda straws - paper clips - string

WHAT TO DO: Stick the paper clips into the ends of 12 straws. Then clip them together to build a cube.

Gently twist the cube down flat into your bubble formula. Lift it out slowly. The bubble will collapse into the center of the cube. Now lower the cube and touch just its bottom to the top of the formula. When you lift it again, you'll have a square bubble in the middle.

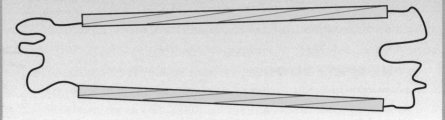

Thread the string through 2 straws. Hold 1 straw in each hand and dip the whole thing in your formula. Lift it out slowly. If you have a friend to help, *You Can* make this loop 5 or 6 feet long. Hold it out tight. Lift it in the wind.

P.S. from Jax: When you're done making bubbles, carefully pour your bubble formula back into the jug. *You Can* use it over and over again.

Dear Joe & Shelley,

That's practically a childhood legend. Everyone has heard that you'd kill a butterfly (or a moth) if you rubbed the *powder* from its wings. But hardly anyone knows why it's actually true.

That *powder* is really tiny little shingles all over the wings – like scales. Without them, the moth or butterfly cannot control its flying. It dies because we've accidentally taken away its ability to find food and shelter.

This is a terrific thing to do a report on at school. *You Can* even make a model of a moth or butterfly wing out of just paper and tape.

Jax Place
Jax Place

25

More Than They Seem

WHAT YOU NEED:
Paper - scissors - tape - crayons

WHAT TO DO: Cut lots of circles. Make them the size of a big coin, like a half-dollar. Then cut them in half. Color them any color you like.

MORE STUFF TO DO: Tape a row of the half-circles across the bottom of another piece of paper. Start a new row above the first, moved over just a bit, like in this drawing. Keep going until the paper is filled. If you like, use the colors to make a pattern.

SO WHAT: Take your project to school and see if anyone can figure out what it's supposed to be. Tell them it's a butterfly wing. When they say you must be really dumb, pull out an encyclopedia and show them a picture to prove it. Blow air over the wing. What happens?

Butterflies — Up Close and Personal

Some schools have microscopes. Some do not. If your school has one, take a moth or a butterfly to class to inspect under the lens. You'll think you're looking at a rooftop covered with shingles. The scales are only on the wing tops.

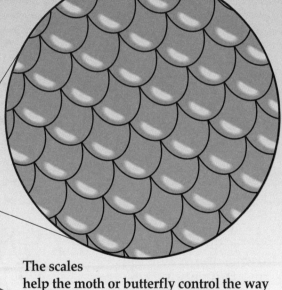

The scales help the moth or butterfly control the way air flows over its wings. Airplanes use flaps called ailerons (AY-leh-ronz) to do the same thing. If moths or butterflies can't fly right, they can't live – so they die.

P.S. from Beakman: All butterflies and moths have a fancy last name — Lepidoptera (lep-eh-DOP-tur-a). It's from 2 Greek words. It means scaly wings!

Dear Beakman,

What is the deal with Christmas lights? Why do some strings just not work?

Flo Mills
Corpus Christi,
Texas

Dear Flo,

Sounds to me like you've had a bad experience with a whole string of tangled lights that refused to shine just because one measly bulb was burned out or was loose.

The deal with Christmas lights is the same with *all electricity* – it has to flow in a loop.

And sometimes lights are wired in a way that makes breaking the loop easier – which makes turning on the lights more difficult.

Beakman

Beakman Place

Tis The Season...

...to get all upset at lights that don't light. Look at the red line. It represents the flow of electrical energy. If just 1 light bulb is loose, the flow of energy is interrupted and the whole string goes out.

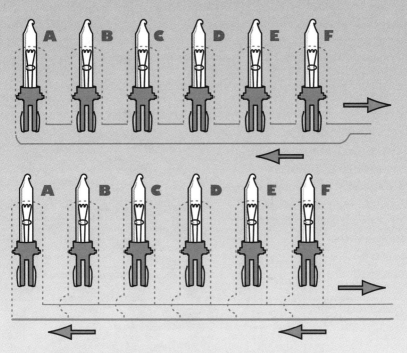

Meanwhile, these bulbs are wired so that the loop is protected no matter what happens to an individual bulb. Bulbs like this cost a bit more. But the aggravation they save is worth it.

P.S. from Jax: The 2 different ways of wiring light bulbs have 2 different names: parallel and series. Use this page to ask your teacher which is which.

29

You Light Up My ~~Life~~ 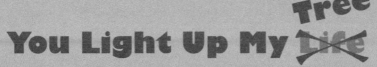 Tree

This kind of light hardly ever messes up. But it's not the shape of the bulb that's important. Instead it's the way the bulbs are connected to each other that makes them easier to light up. Try loosening one or two bulbs from a string of these bulbs, and the rest of the tree will stay lit. That's because they are wired together in a way that protects the loop – the loop electrical energy must flow in.

This mini light is the kind that causes lots of problems. They are usually wired together more simply – which costs less. But it also creates lots more places to break the electrical loop.

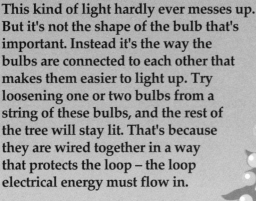

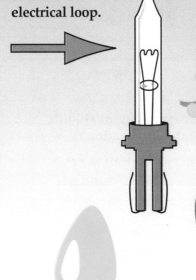

Dear Jax,

What is daylight-saving time? What time is it really?

Leslie Haber
Sacramento,
California

Dear Les,

Hours and minutes and the other ways we measure time were all invented by humans.

You cannot say what time it *really* is because we invented clock time in the first place. Clock time exists only because we all agree on it. Daylight-saving time is just a part of that agreement.

In the spring we agree that sunshine in the early evening is nice, so we all move our clocks ahead. We agree to go to bed an hour earlier and wake up an hour earlier. It means we've changed the numbers we use to describe sunrise and sunset.

Jax Place
Jax Place

31

Remembering

WHAT YOU NEED: Your bed - permission to jump on it - your imagination

WHAT TO DO: Explain to your family that you need a little bit of bed-jumping time for science. They'll probably say yes.

Pretend there's a big *spring* right under your butt. Which way would you go? If you were to *fall* which way would you go? Practice on your bed. *You Can* have fun in bed and be careful and safe at the same time.

SO WHAT: You just learned something *You Can* remember for the rest of your life. Just think of that pretend spring under your rear end.

In the spring, clocks get set forward an hour – just like you would *spring forward* on your bed. In the fall, clocks get set back an hour – just like you would *fall back* in bed.

In 1986 the U.S. Congress made a law that said daylight-saving time would begin in the U.S.A. on the first Sunday in April. That's why lots of people seem confused today.

Night and Day

✂ **Sunset**

WHAT YOU NEED: Tracing paper - toothpick - scissors

WHAT TO DO: Trace the outline and type of figure A, then cut it out. Stick a toothpick through the dot marked B and then through dot C, below.

A

B

Night

Rotate the night disk and put sunrise and sunset where you think they belong.

SO WHAT: Pretty soon you'll see that things like night and day, or sunset and sunrise, are very real things. But the numbers we use to describe these times could change as easy as spinning a disk. The numbers in clock time happen only because we say so and everyone agrees.

Sunrise

When we remember something by playing a trick on ourselves, we call it a mnemonic device (nem-ON-ik). Here's another one: "My very eager mother just served us nine pizzas." The first letters of those words stand for the names of the planets in their proper order, from the sun: Mercury, Venus, Earth, Mars, Jupiter, Saturn, Uranus, Neptune, Pluto.

•C

11 12 1 2 3 4 5 6 7 8 9 10 11 12 1 2 3 4 5 6 7 8 9 10

P.S. from Beakman: Daylight-saving time was invented in England during World War I. The idea spread to North American countries in 1918.

33

Dear Beakman,

Why will an egg float in salt water and won't float in regular water?

Jamie Hoyt
Tacoma,
Washington

Dear Jamie,

The egg-in-salt water trick is sometimes called *magic*. But if you explain a magic trick, it isn't magic anymore. That can make things confusing.

The egg trick is not magic. The answer to your question has to do with *density* (DENS-it-tee).

A floating thing is not as dense as the thing it's floating in. A thing sinks when it's more dense than the thing it sinks in.

Beakman
Beakman Place

Making Water More Dense

WHAT YOU NEED: Salt - water - glass - marking pen

WHAT TO DO: Fill the glass half full of water. Mark the water line with the pen. Stir in as much salt as *You Can* dissolve. It will be a lot – 12 to 15 teaspoons.

Does the water line stay the same? Does it go up by as much salt as you added?

It's Not Magic; It's Real

WHAT YOU NEED: Salt water from Experiment #1 - 2 eggs - 2 glasses - water

WHAT TO DO: Put equal amounts of fresh water and salt water into the 2 glasses. Fill them to be half full.

Now gently place an egg into each of the glasses. The egg in the salt water should float. The egg in the fresh water should sink. It's not magic. The salt water is more dense than the egg, so the egg floats.

What Is Going On

Density matters. A glass of fresh water weighs a certain amount. When you added 12-15 teaspoons of salt, the amount of water did *not* change – the size of the water did *not* change.

What *did change* was the salt made the water heavier. When you make something heavier and keep it the same size, you *increase its density*.

Now your water is salt water and it's *more dense* than fresh water. Salt water is more dense than an egg, so it can hold up an egg. The egg will float.

Fresh water   **Salt water**

Fresh water is not as dense as an egg, so the water cannot hold it up. The egg sinks in fresh water.

P.S. from Jax – It's not just eggs! Ships and everything else that floats will float easier in salt water – even people! Salt water is more dense than fresh water and holds swimmers up better.

Dear Jax,

What is dust and where does it come from?

Scott Rys
Brooklyn,
Minnesota

Dear Scott,

Dust is not just a thing. Dust is a condition. It's a way for something to be – like there's chalk and then there's chalk dust. Also, dust is ubiquitous (u-BICK-kwa-tuss). That means it's everywhere.

House dust is different from true dust. Dust is made from finely powdered rocks and earth.

House dust contains dust and stuff from your house, like lint, paper, hair, pollen and skin cells – your dead skin cells.

Gross but true.

Jax Place
Jax Place

Where Does Dust Come From?

Wind blows across plowed fields, against rocky hills, mud flats or against bare earth. Wind grinds this stuff up into very small pieces. True dust is so small we need to line up 25,000 pieces of it to get just 1 inch.

Wind blowing all over the planet all the time is always making more dust. Dust is so small and light that it floats in air currents. In your house, it swirls around with lint and hair and spider silk and flakes of your skin. When the air is still, it falls and creates a fine layer of house dust on your floors and furniture.

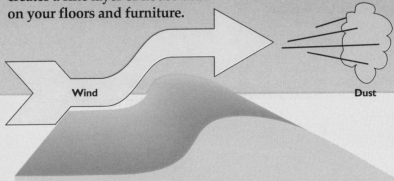

Wind

Dust

Dust: The Good News

Dust Does Affect the Weather

Dust helps it rain or snow. Up in the sky, water vapor gathers as clouds. Dust floating in the air can help water vapor condense into rain. Water condenses on the little pieces of dust. A droplet is formed. Droplets bump into each other and a raindrop is made. It's too heavy to float in a cloud, so it starts to rain. Snow can happen when an ice crystal forms around dust.

Dust helps us get both rain and snow

Dust:
The Bad News
Dust Does Clog Stuff Up

Dust blowing all around all the time gets lots of things dirty.
People in your house may dust the furniture and grumble
about it. No matter how much they gripe, there will always be
more dust. The planet keeps making it.

Our bodies are built to help keep dust out.

Our eyes blink to wash the dust off. The mucus in our nose
blocks out dust. So does the wax in our ears. But some people
are allergic to dust, and dust can make them sick.

Dust Duties

Dust will clog up the air
filter in your heating/
cooling system. This
will make it work
longer and cost more
money. *This is a waste
of energy.* Tell your
family about this, and
help exchange the
filter for a new one.

Find the coils on
your refrigerator.
They will probably
be covered with
dust. Clean them
off. If coils are all gunked
up with dust, the fridge
wastes energy and money.

Furnace filters look like this.

P.S. from Beakman: Microchips are very small electronic circuits; so
small a single piece of dust could wreck them. That's why they're
made in special rooms that are called dust-free. Even then, some
dust does get in.

Dear Beakman,

How do glasses help us to see better?

Laura Hargitt
West Jordan, Utah

Dear Laura,

There are a lot of things our eyes have to do perfectly for us to have perfect sight. If just one of those things is not quite right, we need glasses. But the glasses have to be made just for you and your unique eyes.

Eyeglasses work by bending light beams so that they meet right at the back of our eyeballs on the retina (RET-in-ah). The retina changes light into signals that go to the brain.

Beakman

Beakman Place

A Look Inside Your Looker

A Whole Lot Going On

Our eyeballs work a lot like little cameras. There is a lens that focuses the light. Light has to focus exactly at the retina for our sight to be clear.

The first thing that can go wrong is the length of the eyeball. It can be too short or too long. Or the cornea can have the wrong shape. The lenses in our eyeglasses help the lenses in our eyes. They make sure the light focuses right at the retina so we can see clearly.

When we look at faraway things, the lens is pulled flat by little muscles. When we look at close things, the muscles pull in and the lens gets fat and round. The idea is to keep everything in focus.

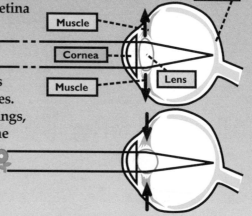

Retina

Muscle

Cornea

Lens

Muscle

EXPERIMENT #1

Different Glasses Fix Different Problems

WHAT YOU NEED: a few friends who wear glasses (perhaps your classmates at school)

WHAT TO DO: Hold a pair of glasses out at the end of your arm. Look at the view. Look at the lenses, too. Look at several different pairs. Be very careful not to hurt the glasses. People who wear glasses need them to see well. Respect that. If you wear glasses, keep yours on when it's your turn.

41

WHAT IS GOING ON:

Different kinds of seeing problems need different kinds of lenses that bend light differently. Here are some examples:

Glasses for farsighted people: These lenses will make the view look bigger or even upside down. When people are farsighted they can see far. They cannot see things clearly that are close up. One cause of it is eyeballs that are too short.

Glasses for nearsighted people: These lenses will make the view look smaller. When people are nearsighted they can see near. They cannot see clearly when things are far away. Their eyeballs may be too long.

Glasses for people with astigmatism: These will change the shape of the view, stretching it out and maybe twisting it. People with astigmatism (ah-STIG-ma-tis-m) have a cornea that is out of shape. The weird stretched-out lens fixes it.

P.S. from Jax: If you know people in their 40s, you may see one of them hold the newspaper at the end of their arms to read. Their lens muscles are weaker and can't focus closely anymore. Mention reading glasses to them.

Dear Beakman,

What are feathers made from?

Marie Schumacher
Kenosha,
Wisconsin

Dear Marie,

On page 58 we talk about animal protein and how it can be turned into glue. On page 154 we talk about zippers. Well, feathers have lots to do with both protein and zippers. An amazing coincidence!

Feathers are made of the same protein our hair is made from, keratin (CARE-eh-tin). Feathers are pretty much *hair with zippers*.

Beakman

Beakman Place

Kinds of Feathers – A Closer Look

WHAT YOU NEED: Feather - feather pillow

WHAT TO DO: *You Can* find a feather on sidewalks or in yards. They're all over the place because birds lose them. Compare one to the tiny fluffy feathers that leak out of a pillow. If you live near a farm, these fluffy feathers can be found near chicken coops or duck ponds. *You Can* even find them leaking out of down sleeping bags or down jackets. Both the feather and the fluff are feathers. But what's the difference? Examine both closely. Compare what's different and the same.

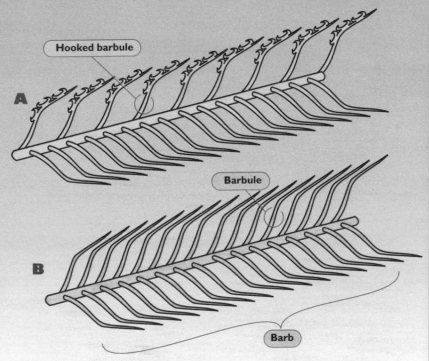

MORE STUFF: Take the larger feather and pull apart the side. Now use your fingers to zip it back together again. Start at the quill and *zipper* out to the edge of the feather.

SO WHAT: Feathers are a lot like hair and fish scales. All are made of keratin. But only feathers have branches that we call *barbs*. Each barb looks like a tiny *feather* itself. These barbs have smaller branches called *barbules* (BAR-byools).

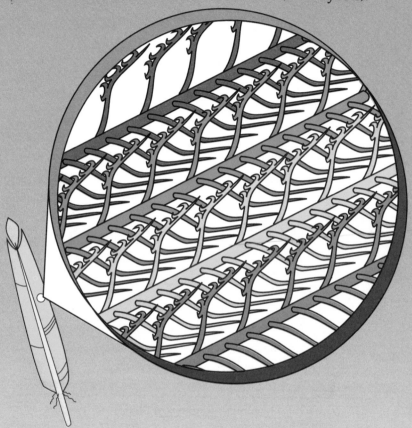

Birds have two different kinds of feathers. The big ones are called *contour feathers*, and the fluffy ones are called *down*. The big difference between them is their barbules. Diagrams A & B are not feathers; they are the branches of feathers. Diagram A is a contour feather barb. Diagram B is down. Down doesn't hook onto itself. It's soft and fluffy. Contour feathers are different. They have hooks on their barbules. The hooks make feathers like hair with zippers. Those hooks are why *You Can* repair a split feather with your fingers.

P.S. from Jax: When you see a bird combing itself with its beak, what it's really doing is zipping its feathers back together again.

Dear Beakman,

Why does fire have so many colors in it?

Kyle Freemantle
Mill Creek,
Washington

Dear Kyle,

In early July, neighbor nations both celebrate holidays that will see lots of colored fire – you know, fireworks.

Canada Day is July 1. In the United States, Independence Day is July 4. Fire changes color because of its temperature. It also changes color when we add certain elements.

And now a warning: ⚠Do NOT conduct any experiments with fire. Fire can destroy your home and even kill you. Ask an adult to help you.

Beakman
Beakman Place

Green Fire?

WHAT YOU NEED: Help from a grown-up - short piece of braided copper wire (like speaker wire) - scissors - gas stove or barbecue - safety glasses

⚠**WHAT NOT TO DO:** *Don't do this without assistance and permission from your family. Stoves and barbecues are dangerous.*

WHAT TO DO: Strip off the plastic insulation from the wire. With the tips of the scissors, snip the fine wires into little bits. This has to be done with great care so that the wire doesn't get into anyone's eyes.

MORE STUFF TO DO: Put the wire bits into a spoon. Pay close attention while an adult tips the wire bits into the gas flame or the barbecue. The flames will briefly turn green.

WHAT IS GOING ON:

Fireworks get their colors from different chemicals burning at very high temperatures. The heat comes from the gunpowder in the fireworks.

In a firework, the most difficult color to make is blue. Blue is made by copper-chloride, but only at a certain temperature. Controlling the temperature is very hard.

White sparkles are made by burning powdered iron.

P.S. from Jax: The flames on a gas stove are blue and very hot because air is mixed into the natural gas before it burns. When your gas stove gets a yellow flame, it means there isn't enough air mixing with the natural gas.

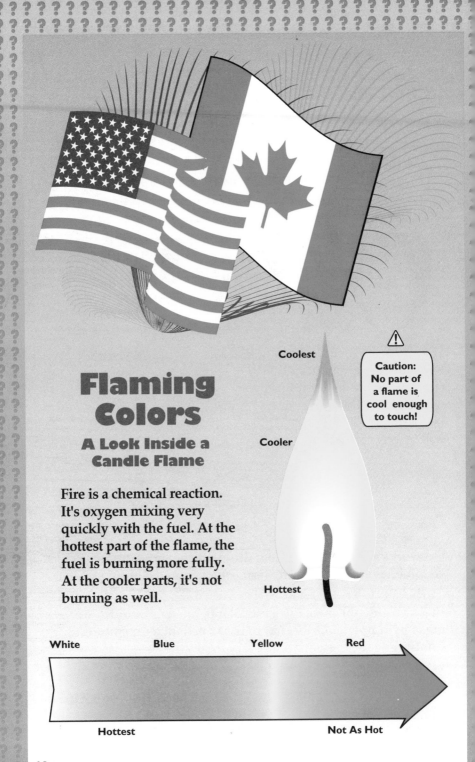

Flaming Colors

A Look Inside a Candle Flame

Fire is a chemical reaction. It's oxygen mixing very quickly with the fuel. At the hottest part of the flame, the fuel is burning more fully. At the cooler parts, it's not burning as well.

Coolest

Cooler

Hottest

⚠️ Caution: No part of a flame is cool enough to touch!

White   Blue   Yellow   Red

Hottest   Not As Hot

Dear Beakman,

How do fossils turn into rocks?

Chad Conley
Chicago, Illinois

Dear Chad,

Fossils are like the planet's scrapbook.
Things get saved and sometimes hidden
or forgotten in a scrapbook. When we find
them again, these bits and pieces of life's
leftovers are full of clues about our past. It's
the same with fossils.

But fossils are not things that have turned
into rock. Most fossils are rocks that were
made in the shape of a living thing that
decayed and left behind a mold – a mold in
the living thing's shape.

You Can use plaster to make a fossil in a few
minutes. Real fossils take many thousands
of years to form.

Beakman

Beakman Place

Make a Fossil

EXPERIMENT #1

WHAT YOU NEED: Plaster of Paris - petroleum jelly - old baking pan - help from a grown-up

WHAT TO DO: Slime up one of your hands with the petroleum jelly. Mix enough plaster to put about an inch into an old baking pan. Gently press your hand into the plaster until you have just dented the plaster's surface. ⚠️*Caution: Do not push your hand all the way into the plaster. You could get stuck.* Plaster makes heat when it cures, so expect the pan to get warm. Since your hand will be on top of the plaster, *You Can* just lift it off if it gets too warm for comfort.

MORE STUFF TO DO: Leave your hand in place until the plaster cures – 15-20 minutes. After it's hard, slime up the plaster handprint you just made. Cover it with greasy petroleum jelly. Mix up another batch of plaster and pour it on top of your handprint. After the new plaster cures, pop them apart. If it won't pop open, stand it up on the edge and tap it lightly with a hammer.

Finding Fossils

This is a fossil of an ammonite (AM-en-ite). Remember, this is not a shell that turned into rock. Rather it is a rock that was deposited in the shape of an ancient animal. *You Can* find fossils all around. You just have to look closely at lots of rocks.

A great thing to look at is limestone driveway gravel. Look very closely and you'll find little fossils of sea shells in the bits of gravel. They are a lot like the plaster hand you made in the second part of your experiment.

P.S. from Jax: Believe it or not, the fossil of your hand is very important to your family. Present it as a gift. It'll be a fossil of you. And as the years pass, it will become a more valued relic of your life.

Dear Michelle,

Television is really radio waves carrying both sound and pictures. Radio waves are carefully controlled electromagnetic radiation.

The electric motor in your mixer makes lots and lots of electric sparks as it spins. And all sparks make electromagnetic radiation. Sometimes we call this radiation RF, which stands for *radio frequency*.

Your TV picks up the RF from the TV station and also the RF from the mixer. The mixer's RF is not controlled and is all mixed up. That's what messes up your TV.

Jax Place
Jax Place

The sparks inside this mixer make wild and crazy radio waves –
RF – so crazy that the TV picture will roll and be crazy itself.
The noise you'll hear in your experiment is turned into a
picture on TV. That's what is meant by the term *noisy image*.

P.S. from Beakman: The word radiation can sometimes confuse you.
Radiation means when something radiates from one location
outward – like light from a light bulb. Not all radiation is unsafe. The
dangerous kind is called ionizing radiation.

53

Get Some Sparks Going

WHAT YOU NEED: Small appliances with motors and permission to use them - AM radio

WHAT TO DO: Tune the radio to what I call *Zen radio*. I mean, tune so that you can't hear any station clearly. Tune to *no station*. Turn on the appliances one by one; change their speeds; turn them on in groups. Listen to the sounds the radio makes.

SO WHAT:

You heard lots of rapid clicking, and the speed of the clicks changed as the speed of the motors changed. If you look in the vent holes of some appliances, you can even see sparking as it happens.

The invention of the radio happened after people began paying attention to sparks and what they do. This means your Mixmaster is really a little, out-of-control radio station!

If you invent a code, *You Can* send messages to your friends on Zen radio with an appliance.

54

Dear Jax,

What are ghosts besides scary and gloomy?

Rachel Cameron
Waterloo,
Belgium

Dear Rachel,

Your terrific question shows us all that there are limits to what can be known and explained for sure.

Some things are either believed or not believed without any proof or reason. That's how it is with ghosts.

Maybe only humans can have or believe in ghosts because humans have something very special and wonderful – an imagination. Since we cannot prove anything about ghosts, let's talk about that – our imaginations – and what ghosts *might* be.

Jax Place
Jax Place

The Strength of Imagination

WHAT YOU NEED: Quiet time with yourself - pillow

WHAT TO DO: Lie down on your back somewhere that you like – a yard, a park or your room. Close your eyes and get peaceful-like. Decide to take yourself someplace else. *Notice everything* around you – the feel of the ground or your bed, the sounds, the temperature. Imagine you have all of those feelings in a new place. What would the new place be? What would you do there? What would it be like? Who are you in this new place?

WHAT IS GOING ON:

Talk about power! You just invented a whole new world all by yourself. Sometimes it's called a daydream, and daydreams are very important. They give your imagination room to stretch and grow. They give you ideas that you can't get anyplace else. They can help you solve problems of all kinds.

The next time someone tells you to stop daydreaming, you might tell them you're working on your imagination and it's working on you.

Ghosts – The Decision Is Yours

OK, so we know that *You Can* invent any reality you want with the powers of your imagination. Our imagination is certainly able to invent a few pretend ghosts to prowl around our rooms at night.

Still, many people say that the ghosts they've seen are *not* their imagination. Many others say ghosts do not exist at all. This makes things hard. The difficulty is deciding what is real without taking power away from your imagination. You don't want to make your imagination weak, because it's a very important thing.

Something that might help you decide is to help someone else. A friend or people in your family might get scared. They might tell you they've seen a ghost, or a monster in their room. Tell them that it's terrific, fantastic and wonderful!

Ask them to show you and tell you all about it. *Don't ever* tell them, "It was *just* your imagination." Instead, tell them it's great that we can all see things in our own personal way. Sooner or later, the same thing will happen to you – you'll get scared. And then, you'll have to decide for yourself – was it a ghost, a personal vision, both or neither?

P.S. from Beakman: When we can't prove something but have some clues about it, we call that a theory (**THEER**-ee). Experiments are done to see if the clues are right. If an experiment doesn't work, we have to take a new look at things.

Dear Crystal,

Glue works because it fits exactly between the things you're gluing together. When glue dries, it leaves behind a bridge between those surfaces.

All of this is happening on a very small scale, so we have to use the M word – molecular. The bridges are really protein molecules anchored at each end by the thing you're gluing. Glue is made out of animal protein – usually an impure form of gelatin – and something liquid in which to dissolve the protein. Usually that's water.

Everything else that sticks is not really glue. It's an adhesive.

Jax Place

Jax Place

EXPERIMENT #1

Make Some Glue

WHAT YOU NEED: 2 cups *skim* milk - 4 tsp. vinegar - 4 tsp. baking soda - help from a grown-up - wire sieve - frying pan - warm water

WHAT TO DO: Heat the milk and the vinegar in the pan. Stir constantly until the milk turns into lumps. Strain out the liquid and save the lumps in a bowl. Add 2 tablespoons warm water and smash in the baking soda with a fork. Watch it fizz.

Dump the glue into your sieve and force it through the little wires into a jar.

Let it sit on a shelf, covered up, for a whole day. Now stir it up again. You've just made casein (KAY-seen) glue. Casein is a protein in milk. *You Can* use your glue for paper or wood.

P.S. from Beakman: When you added the vinegar to the milk, you made something from a nursery rhyme — the one about Little Miss Muffett. You made curds (the lumps) and whey (the clear liquid).

How It Works

The water carries the protein into all the nooks and crannies in these 2 pieces of wood. Then the water dries, which leaves the protein molecules behind. As the protein dries, it forms bridge-like patterns between the 2 pieces of wood.

We say that the protein has a structure. Before the structure could form, the glue flowed to fill the space between the wood completely.

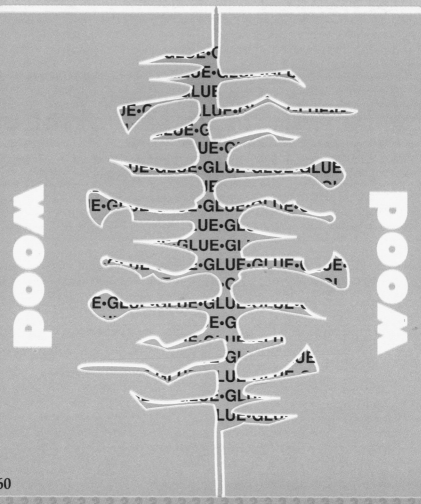

Dear Jax,

What are goose bumps? Where do they come from?

Callie Wilson
Columbus, Ohio

Dear Callie,

Talking about goose bumps means talking about something controversial (con-tra-VUR-shul). When something is controversial, people think different things about the same subject and talk about it a lot. So here goes.

We get goose bumps because of *evolution* (ev-eh-LU-shun). Evolution is a thing some people don't believe in. But many people – like me – do believe it. That makes it controversial.

Evolution is a theory that says living things change over time as their environments change.

Jax Place
Jax Place

Goose Bumps: Evolution in Action

Goose bumps are all about insulation and keeping warm. When fur is all fluffed up, it's a better insulator. It's better at keeping out the cold. Humans aren't covered with fur. But our prehistoric, pre-human ancestors probably were. This is the evolution part.

When it got cold, their fur stood on end, trapping air and forming an insulation barrier. Our goose bumps are sort of a leftover from those days – millions of years ago.

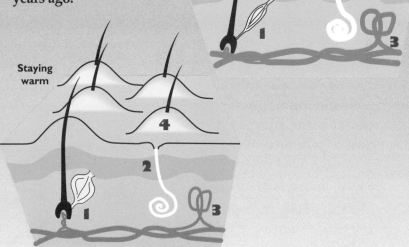

Cooling off

Staying warm

When it's hot, little muscles at each hair (1) relax. Your hair is relaxed. Your sweat glands (2) pump out body heat in sweat. Your blood vessels (3) get big to take more heat to the skin to get rid of it.

When it's cold, the arrector muscle (1) pulls the hair up. The duct to the sweat glands (2) gets small to conserve heat. Our blood vessels (3) get small to save heat. Hair standing up doesn't make good insulation anymore – we don't have enough fur for that. But it does make goose bumps (4).

Goose Bumps on Purpose

WHAT YOU NEED: Just yourself –
and the time to notice a few things

WHAT TO DO: The next time you take a bath or a shower, pay closer attention to what's happening.

After the shower is off, or you're out of the tub, step into the center of the room. Don't grab a towel. Relax with your arms at your sides. Take a deep, deep breath. Let it *all out slowly*. What happened?

WHAT IS GOING ON: You just had a reflexive event. *Reflex* means it happens without you having to make it happen. The body reacts on its own. As you let out that deep breath, you relaxed and gave up some muscle control. You probably had a big shiver.

Your muscles shivered on their own. The reason for the muscles doing that is to *make more body heat*. Believe it or not, your goose bumps are also about getting warm.

P.S. from Beakman: Cold is not the only thing that can cause our hair to stand on end. Fear or anger can cause the same reflex. The same is true for other mammals. You'll notice that on a cat or dog.

Dear Beakman,

Why is the grass green?

Melanie Lizcano
San Antonio,
Texas

Dear Melanie,

Grass and other plants are little, solar-powered chemical factories. They take carbon dioxide from the air plus water from their roots and turn them into oxygen as well as a simple kind of sugar that plants use for food.

There is a chemical that is needed for this all to work. It's called chlorophyll (KLOR-a-fill) and without it, the sunshine cannot take apart and build new molecules. Chlorophyll is bright green.

The green in grass and trees and all plants is from that green chemical, chlorophyll.

You Can grow little plants to watch chlorophyll work.

Beakman

Beakman Place

One From Column A

EXPERIMENT #1

WHAT YOU NEED: Empty jar with lid - dried beans - hammer and nail - family permission or assistance - patience

WHAT TO DO: Remove any lid liners and punch lots and lots of holes through the lid. This is the dangerous part. (You can't believe the angry letters I get when I tell you guys to use a hammer. So, watch out! Be safe.)

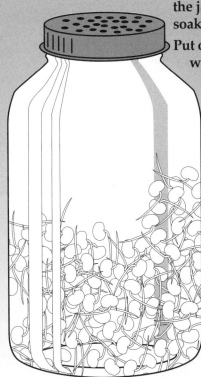

MORE STUFF: Pour in the beans till you've added about 1 inch. Fill the jar with water and let the beans soak for about 6 hours.

Put on the lid and dump out the water through the holes.

Put the jar in a completely dark place, like a closed cupboard. Every day open the jar, add water, and dump it out through the holes in the lid. Return the jar to the dark cupboard.

In 4 days the jar will be filled with sprouts.

So What

Your beans look something like this. They are still getting the food they need from the seed. As soon as that food runs out, the sprouts will have to power up their chemical factories and start turning water and carbon dioxide into sugar and oxygen. They'll power it all with just sunshine.

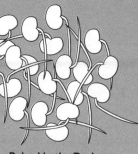

Raised in the Dark

To see it, put your jar of sprouts in the daylight for an afternoon. The next time you look at them, the sprouts will have powered up.

In a couple hours, the sprouts will turn green. That's because they begin to make chlorophyll, which they'll need to start making food. The same thing happens with grass.

Let the Sun Shine In

You Can turn off the grass's chemical factory by putting a board on the lawn for several days. When you lift it up again, the grass underneath will be yellowish or white.

By the way, your bean sprouts are excellent eating. Try them on a sandwich or in a salad.

P.S. from Jax: Mushrooms are not green because they do not have to be. They don't make their own food, so they don't need chlorophyll. Mushrooms live on food other plants make.

Dear Beakman,

What's the deal with hair? How does it grow?

Bessie Mathewson
Douglas,
Arizona

Dear Bessie,

All mammals have hair – including humans. Hair is a thread of dead protein called keratin (KAIR-eh-tin) and it's all over the place.

We have tiny soft hairs just about every place on our body. There are places with no hair at all, like the palms of our hands and the bottoms of feet. Then there is heavier hair – like on our heads.

I hate the idea of anything being *average*. But the average head has 100,000 separate hairs on it. At any one time 5,000 to 15,000 of them are taking a rest from growing. We lose 70 to 100 of those resting hairs a day.

Beakman
Beakman Place

67

Make Really Big Hair

WHAT YOU NEED: Paper plates - tape - cardboard tube

WHAT TO DO: Tape the paper plates onto the tube. Start at one end and work your way to the other, making scales.

With your hand loosely on the tube, stroke up and then down the plates.

WHAT IS GOING ON: Stroke your own hair in both directions. Just like your model big hair, it's rough one way and smooth the other. It's the scales on your hairs that make them seem rough. When people comb their hair the wrong direction, all the scales bend and break outward and the hairs will stick to each other. It damages your hair. The name for it tells you a lot – *ratting hair*.

EXPERIMENT #1

EXPERIMENT #2

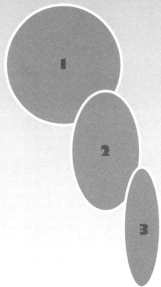

WHAT YOU NEED: Soda straw

WHAT TO DO: Try to make the straw wavy or curly.

WHAT IS GOING ON: You have to flatten the straw to wave or curl it.

1-Straight hair is round.

2-Wavy hair is slightly flattened.

3-Curly hair is nearly flat.

Inside Hair

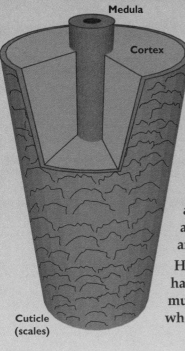

Medula

Cortex

Cuticle (scales)

Hair grows upward from the root area. The dead zone is where the living hair dies and turns into hard keratin. Above that zone, the hair shaft is dead.

The sebaceous (sa-BAY-shus) glands make oil that coats our hair and keeps all the little scales closed and sealed. That makes hair soft and shiny.

Hair color is in the cortex. Gray hair has no color at all. The arrector muscle pulls hair up on end – like when we get a goose bump.

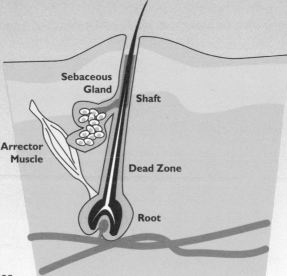

Sebaceous Gland

Shaft

Arrector Muscle

Dead Zone

Root

If hair strands were really big, they would look a little like fish – covered with scales.

P.S. from Jax: I have bright pink hair. My brother, Beakman, has blue hair. Hair in those colors exists only in the funnies, or if you use very radical hair dye.

Dear Beakman,

How does the human heart work?

Debra Judelson
Beverly Hills,
California

Dear Rachel,

Thank you for your letter and the excellent question.

The human heart is a big set of muscles about the size of your fist. It's a pump that moves blood through miles of veins and arteries. That blood feeds all of the body's cells, removes cell waste and defends us against invaders like germs.

A pump is usually a machine with a set of pistons or a propeller-like set of blades. But the heart has none of those. It's basically a hollow, ball-like muscle.

You Can copy the pumping action of the heart in this experiment.

Beakman

Beakman Place

How Can a Ball of Muscle Be a Pump?

WHAT YOU NEED: An empty squeeze bottle with a closing top, like a dish soap bottle

WHAT TO DO: The next time you take a bath, take a few minutes to turn your dish soap bottle into a pump. Before you get in the tub, ask someone who's allowed to use a knife to cut a small hole in the bottom of the bottle.

You have to be able to cover the hole with your finger.

First, hold the bottle under water and fill it with water. Put the cap on and pull the top so that it's open. Hold one finger over the little hole and lift the top out of the water. The bottom of the bottle is still underwater. With the hole covered, squeeze the bottle.

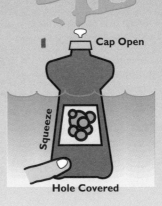

I   Cap Open

Squeeze

Hole Covered

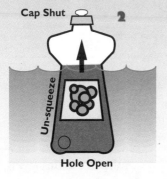

Cap Shut   **2**

Un-squeeze

Hole Open

Keep squeezing the bottle and lift your finger off the hole. With the bottle still squeezed, shut the top of the cap. Now let the bottle expand. When it's full, cover the little hole with your finger again and open the cap.

Now you can start over again.

71

What Is Going On

Your squeeze bottle behaved a lot like the heart. It got bigger and smaller and sucked in and squeezed out bath water. The heart does the same thing with blood.

Our hearts are divided into four chambers. Chambers A and B are called atriums (A-tree-umz). C and D are called ventricles (VEN-tree-culz). They squeeze and un-squeeze to pump blood.

Your experiment and your heart wouldn't work without valves. In your tub, the valves were your finger on the hole and the cap. In our heart, the valves are little flaps of muscle that open and close. In this simplified drawing, the valves have circles around them. The valves make sure that blood (or bath water) goes in only one direction.

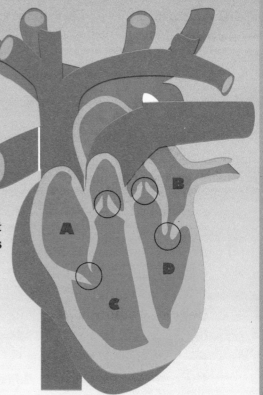

P.S. from Jax: Your heart beats all the time for your whole life. An adult's heart beats 60 to 80 times a minute. A child's heart beats 80 to 100 times a minute.

Dear Jax,

How do bees make honey?

Stacey Nutt
Ames, Iowa

Dear Stacey,

When it's Saint Valentine's Day and lots of people are calling each other *honey*, it's a great time to tell everyone that honey is flower nectar that bees throw up. It's not vomit, but it's something that bees *do* throw up anyway.

When it's cold, bees eat food they've stored for the winter months. They eat honey and bee bread – which isn't really bread. It's flower pollen mixed with bee spit.

If it's cold where you live, you might enjoy a nice warm cup of honey-cocoa today. In fact, *You Can* make it for your special *honey*.

Jax Place
Jax Place

Bee My Honey — Or Bee a Honey to Someone Else

EXPERIMENT #1

WHAT YOU NEED: Unsweetened cocoa powder - milk - honey - spices like cinnamon, allspice or cloves - permission to cook

WHAT TO DO: Heat up $1\frac{1}{2}$ cups milk for every mug of cocoa you want to make. Just as the milk boils, add the spices – as much as you like – and remove from the heat. Stir in 1 tablespoon cocoa and 2 tablespoons of honey for every mug of cocoa you're making. Whip it up really well and share with your Valentine's Day honey.

MORE BEE STUFF: Bees sting to defend their hive. They do not sting to defend themselves. How do we know that? Well, when a bee stings you, the stinger (c) is ripped out of the bee's rear end. It leaves a gaping wound that

usually kills the bee. It doesn't make much sense for the bee to die defending itself.

It can make sense if you think about the whole beehive as one living thing – made from many hundred single bees. Several bees may die defending the hive, but the community is still alive.

Honey: Not a Pretty Story

Worker bees have to fly about 50,000 miles to gather enough nectar to make just 1 pound of honey.

A bee sucks up nectar from flowers with its long tongue (a).

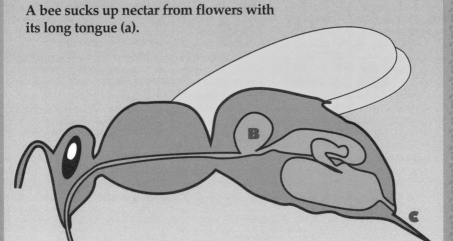

It swallows flower nectar, which goes to a special stomach (b) just for storing nectar. When the bee gets back to the hive, another bee – presumably a friend – sticks its tongue down the first bee's throat and sucks the nectar out of the honey-stomach.

The new bee lets the nectar ripen into honey in its honey-stomach and then throws up into a wax chamber in the honeycomb. Yum!

P.S. from Beakman: Killer bees are really just bees that get angry quickly, which is a big problem with a whole hive of them. But just one killer bee cannot hurt you any more than one regular honeybee.

75

Dear Jax,

What is a horoscope?

Michael Uttamchandani
Winnipeg, Manitoba

Dear Michael,

The word horoscope means to *watch time*. It's a kind of chart that explains where certain planets were when someone was born. It's part of something called *astrology*, which has lots of math, charts and geometry, making it look like science. But it isn't really science.

The basic belief of astrology is that the stars and planets and their positions in the sky affect life here on Earth – and that by measuring these positions you can reveal behavior and predict the future.

As absurd as that might sound, lots of people believe or just enjoy astrology. One example is former President Ronald Reagan, whose wife used to arrange the time he would sign treaties and hold meetings all according to astrology.

Jax Place

A Little Empirical Research Project for You

Does It Work?

WHAT YOU NEED: Newspapers - notebook - pencils or pens

WHAT TO DO: Start keeping a journal. Sometimes it's called a diary. (If you call it a journal, people will take it more seriously, and I don't know why.) Anyway, write down the really big stuff every day and make notes on how you felt about it.

Cut out the astrology column from the newspaper every day. But don't read it. Put the date on it and fold it in half.

WHAT IS GOING ON: In a week or so, go back and read your journal and then read the astrology columns with it. Do they match? Probably not. But sometimes they might. And that is the thing that gives scientists a hard time. As silly as astrology seems, you can defend it by saying that every once in a while it seems to work!

By the way, *empirical* means to learn from direct experience.

What's Your Sign?

Aries (The Ram)
March 21 - April 19

Libra (The Scales)
Sept. 23 - Oct. 22

Taurus (The Bull)
April 20 - May 20

Scorpio (Scorpion)
Oct. 23 - Nov. 21

Gemini (The Twins)
May 21 - June 20

Sagittarius
(Archer-Centaur)
Nov. 22 - Dec. 21

Cancer (The Crab)
June 21 - July 22

Capricorn (Goat)
Dec. 22 - Jan. 19

Leo (The Lion)
July 23 - August 22

Aquarius (The
Water Carrier)
Jan. 20 - Feb. 18

Virgo (The Virgin)
August 23 - Sept. 22

Pisces (The Fish)
Feb. 19 - March 20

to introduce themselves by explaining their sign and then saying they

for zodiac signs. Find your birthday, and then learn how to make the sy

Astrologers use these symbols

could tell what sign you were!

P.S. from Beakman: The disease cancer is named after the astrological sign for the crab — Cancer. That's because the first tumors studied looked like little crabs, with many arms reaching outward.

Dear Beakman,

Why is a knife sharp?

Katie Krause
Staples,
Minnesota

Dear Katie,

Knives provide many challenges. First there's the weird way you spell their name. Then there are the dangers. After all, the whole idea of a knife is to cut things. And you do not want to cut yourself.

Knives are about force and concentrating force. The reason a knife is sharp is that a very fine point concentrates force – enough force to slice things apart.

The opposite of how a knife works is a bed of nails. It has nothing to do with being in a trance. It does have to do with spreading the force out.

Beakman

Beakman Place

Concentrating the Force

EXPERIMENT #1

WHAT YOU NEED:
Cereal boxtop - stick of butter or margarine

WHAT TO DO: Lay the boxtop flat on the butter. Now push down. Next, stand the boxtop on its edge and push down. What happened?

WHAT IS GOING ON: The flat boxtop would not cut into the butter. Your force down was spread out over the whole width of the boxtop. On its edge, the boxtop concentrated your force and sliced the butter. The smaller the edge, the more it concentrates the same force.

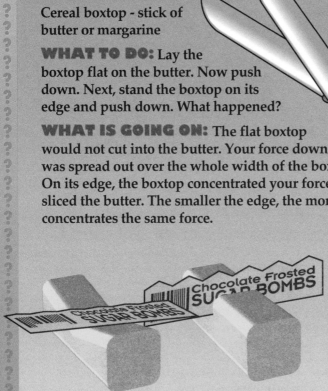

KNIFE NOTICE
⚠ Warning: Knives are *extremely dangerous*. The idea here is to explain them only. Never touch a knife without family permission.

Spreading Force Out

EXPERIMENT #2

WHAT YOU NEED: Balloon - straight pins - shoe box - graph paper - brick - permission and help from your family

WHAT TO DO: Tape down the graph paper on the bottom of the box. Stick 1 pin every place 2 lines cross. When you turn the box over, it should be full of pins sticking straight up. Blow up the balloon and place it in the box on the pins. Balance the brick on the balloon.

WHAT IS GOING ON:

The force of the brick was spread out over dozens and dozens of pins. There wasn't enough pressure on any one pin to burst the balloon. This is a safe model of the bed-of-nails-trick that people can get all mystical about.

P.S. from Jax: Concentration of force is why high-heeled shoes sink into soft dirt. All the weight is concentrated on those teeny little heels.

Dear Beakman,

Why do knuckles crack?

Pamela Stamm
Paw Paw,
Michigan

Dear Pamela,

Sometimes, very little things make a lot of noise. A baby brother or sister, a kernel of popcorn, and your knuckles are all small, and all can make lots of sound.

Your knuckles don't pop or crack. What's making the sound is a tiny bubble of gas escaping from the liquid inside your joints.

That liquid is a kind of joint lube. In one way, it's like soda pop. It has a gas dissolved in it.

Beakman

Beakman Place

More Space = More Bubbles

WHAT YOU NEED: Half-full bottle of soda, the kind with a screw top.

WHAT TO DO: With the top on tight, shake the bottle. Wait until it stops fizzing and shake it again. Keep doing that until there is no more fizzing.

Slowly and carefully unscrew the top. Make sure to look at the soda when you do this.

WHAT IS GOING ON: When you released the pressure, you created the space for more bubbles to come out of the soda. The same thing would happen if you somehow could make the closed bottle bigger.

That's a lot like your knuckles – a fluid with gas dissolved.

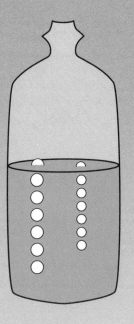

Big Sounds from Little Bubbles

WHAT YOU NEED: Chewing gum

WHAT TO DO: Chew up the gum till it's soft. Use your tongue to flatten out the gum and fold it over inside your mouth. Then move it over to the side of your mouth and bite down hard on the bubble inside the folded gum. This may take practice, but you'll soon be making a very loud (and annoying) sound.

A Look Inside

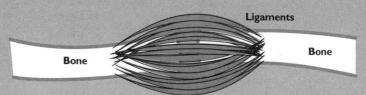

If you've ever taken apart chicken bones, you know that they aren't connected to each other. Bones are held together by ligaments.

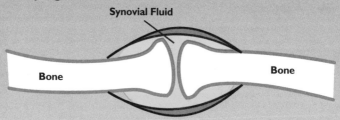

If we could look inside, we'd see a droplet of synovial fluid (se-NO-vee-ul) between the bones. The fluid is held in tight by the ligaments and is under lots of pressure.

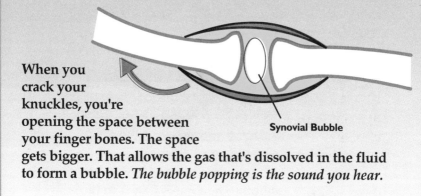

When you crack your knuckles, you're opening the space between your finger bones. The space gets bigger. That allows the gas that's dissolved in the fluid to form a bubble. *The bubble popping is the sound you hear.*

P.S. from Jax – An important question doesn't seem to have one answer: Is it bad for you to crack your knuckles? Different people say different things. I guess you have to decide yourself.

Dear Jax,

How does a laser work?

Aaron Bielinski
Green Bay,
Wisconsin

Dear Aaron,

Lasers work because atoms get all excited and spit out light. All this excitement happens in between two mirrors that are a lot like those mirrored sunglasses Michael Jackson always wears.

We use laser light to play CDs, to scan those bar code things at the grocery store, and even to make phone calls. Laser light carries our calls through miles of thin strands of glass.

Jax Place
Jax Place

Fiber Optics at Home

WHAT YOU NEED: Small jar with lid - long black sock - flashlight - the kitchen sink - nail - hammer - darkness

WHAT TO DO: Punch 2 holes in the lid of the jar. Put the flashlight all the way into the bottom of the sock. Fill the jar with water and put on the lid. Slide the jar into the sock.

Turn off the lights. Turn on the flashlight. Now pour the water into your sink.

SO WHAT: Light travels in straight lines. That means your experiment should shine light along the line marked A. But it doesn't. Your light shone along line B. You just bent a beam of light around a corner. This is exactly how we can use laser light to send telephone calls down a long, curvy fiber of glass. Inside strands of glass and in streams of water, the light bounces off the inside walls. No matter which way the strand or stream bends, the light will follow it, bouncing along inside.

Tickle City

That's How a Laser Works.

To understand lasers, you have to use your imagination. Imagine you're in a funhouse with your friends and you're all locked inside a bouncy rubber room. Now, one of you starts a tickling fight. The tickling grows until you're all doing it and you're all bouncing off the wall laughing like crazy. It gets so wild in there that you bust right out through one of the walls. That's sort of how a laser works, only it happens with atoms, and instead of laughter, they give off pure uniform light.

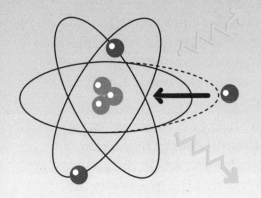

Light from a flash tube excites the atoms in a rod of ruby crystal. The orbit of the electrons can jump out.

When the orbit jumps back down, the atom can release light. This light is bounced between mirrors on the end of the rod and causes other atoms to release light. The light gets so intense it breaks through the mirrors, just like some sunlight gets through Michael's sunglasses.

P.S. from Beakman: Laser light is special because its light waves are in sync with each other. That means the light will not spread out like other light and can focus lots of energy tightly.

Dear Beakman,

Why do tree leaves turn colors in the fall?

Aaron Weir
Circle Pines,
Minnesota

Dear Aaron,

Lots of people want the answer to that question. More than 150 people have asked me that same question. Your letter got here first, so your name is in the book. But the answer is for everyone!

Here's the big surprise: Leaves do not change color in the fall. Instead, leaves *lose one color* (green). The new color you see in the fall was always there. It's just that the green was too strong a pigment to let it show.

Beakman
Beakman Place

A Closer Look

These are ginkgo tree leaves. They're pretty in the fall. Look at the yellow leaf. It is the very same picture as the green leaf. The only difference is, I've removed the green.

That's exactly what's happening on real trees. The chemical that's green is called chlorophyll (KLOR-o-fill).

In the fall the tree stops using chlorophyll. The chemicals that are left behind can then be seen. Yellow comes from a chemical called xanthophyll (ZAN-tho-fill).

Xanthophyll (yellow). By itself, yellow can be seen.

Xanthophyll (yellow) plus chlorophyll (green). The green is so strong, we can't see the yellow.

Trees use their leaves to make simple sugars. We've looked at that process before in *You Can.*

It's when trees take carbon dioxide from the air and water from the ground and turn it into sugar and oxygen. An important chemical in that process is the one that makes leaves green, chlorophyll.

When the fall comes and the days get shorter, some trees can't make enough sugar with the shorter daylight hours and shut down their sugar factories.

Leaf Colors

Here is a chart of 3 leaf colors: red, yellow and green.

If all are in a leaf together, the color is deep green (center).

Remove the green and you get reds, yellows and oranges.

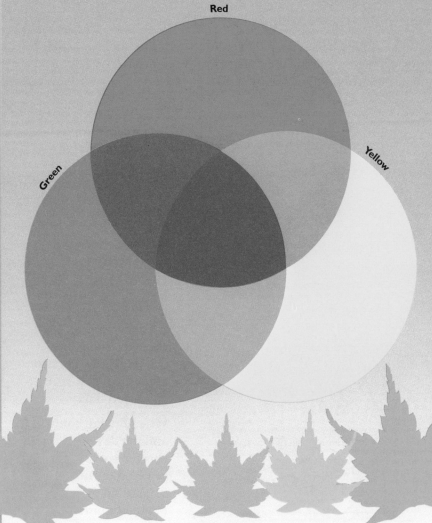

P.S. from Jax: The next time you get a grass stain on a white shirt or pants, look carefully at the colors. In addition to the green, *You Can* also see some yellow. If someone complains about the stains, tell them you were doing scientific research.

Dear Jax,

How do levers make you stronger?

Eric Barther
Tel Aviv,
Israel

Dear Eric,

Levers do not make you stronger. A lever helps you do more work with the strength you already have. They work so well, *You Can* lift a whole car with just one hand – if you have the right lever.

A lever is a basic machine. All tools are combinations of the basic machines. Basic machines are things like: a wheel, a screw, an incline, a pulley or a lever.

Levers are all over your house. And *You Can* see how they work with today's experiments.

Jax Place
Jax Place

Levers
(Lee-Vurs or Lev-urz?)

The fulcrum (FULL-krum) is the place a lever rocks back and forth. You could call it a pivot.

When it's right in the middle of the lever, the amount of work you push down equals exactly the amount of load you can lift with the other end.

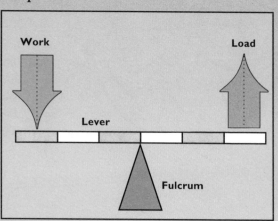

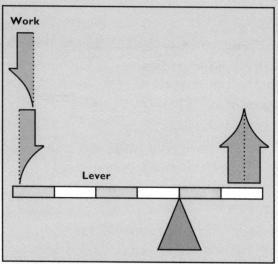

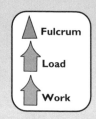

Now the fulcrum is closer to the load. The distance from the work end to the fulcrum is twice the distance from the fulcrum to the load. That seems to increase your strength. You only have to push down half as hard to lift the same weight.

The difference is you have to push down a longer distance.

Putting Levers to Work

EXPERIMENT #1

Pound a nail almost all the way into some wood. Use your fingers to pull it out. Now try pulling it out with the hammer. It's a lot easier. The claw on a hammer is a lever. We call this kind of lever a first-class lever. It does not mean it's a better lever – just that it's the first *kind* of lever.

EXPERIMENT #2

Use your first finger and thumb to pop off a metal cap from a soda bottle. Don't twist it off, pry it off. Now try a bottle opener. Much easier, right? A bottle opener is a second-class lever, which means the fulcrum is at the end of the lever and the load is in the middle.

EXPERIMENT #3

A third-class lever has its fulcrum at one end and the load at the other end, with the work you do in the middle. It's how a fishing pole works. You lift just a short distance at the handle, but the end of the pole pops up several feet – hopefully with dinner on the line.

P.S. from Beakman: *You Can lift a car with a jack, which is a first-class lever.* Other levers include nail clippers, wheelbarrows, baseball bats, pliers, scissors and lots more.

Dear Jax,

How do locks in doorknobs work?

Kelly Ausburn
Seattle,
Washington

Dear Kelly,

The kind of lock we use most was invented almost 4,000 years ago by the Egyptians. They had lots of expensive things they wanted to keep safe – you know, jewels and mummies.

The padlock is a *portable lock*. It was invented later by the Romans, who went around conquering stuff and then locking it up.

The lock you're interested in works by stopping the knob from turning. *You Can* build a simple model to learn what's going on inside.

Jax Place
Jax Place

Lock It Up

WHAT YOU NEED: 2 paper cups - 3 pencils

WHAT TO DO: Put 1 cup inside the other and twist them back and forth. Now imagine that one cup is the doorknob and the other cup is the hole in the door. The knob twists in the door, and it's unlocked.

Next, stick three pencils through the side of the nested cups. Now try to twist the cups. Take out the pencils and twist.

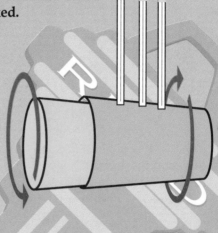

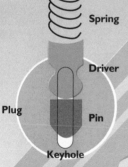

Spring

Driver

Plug

Pin

Keyhole

WHAT IS GOING ON:
I know that seemed simple and everything, but that's how a lock works. In a lock, the pencils are called pins and drivers, and they're all different lengths.

A key's teeth pushes them to just the right place, and the knob is free to twist. The diagram on page 96 explains it better.

95

Key Facts

Most door locks have five sets of drivers/pins. The pins can be any length. The key has to match each and every pin-length or else the plug cannot rotate. The pins are like your pencils. If just one pencil stays in your cups, they are still locked.

The key has pushed the pins and drivers up. Now they all match, and the plug can turn. The door is unlocked.

Unlocked

Locked

The driver has been pushed up by the key. The pin and the plug can now rotate freely.

Ramses II – Pharaoh

P.S. from Beakman – Since there are five pins and each one is a different length, there are thousands and thousands of different keys that could be made. That's why your key doesn't work at a friend's house. The pins aren't the same.

Dear Beakman,

Can you show us how You Can make hand lotion?

Cheryl Castator
Bramalea,
Ontario

Dear Cheryl,

You're thinking big! Lotions, creams and makeup are not what you might think. They are *not* about beauty shops and beauty operators.

They are about chemists and laboratories. If you don't believe me, read the list of ingredients on any cosmetics package – like shampoo, shave cream or soap. *Try reading it out loud.*

Two famous women chemists' names can be found on cosmetics – Helena Rubenstein and Estee Lauder. Maybe soon, we'll read Cheryl Castator alongside them.

Beakman

Beakman Place

Homemade Hand Lotion

WHAT YOU NEED: Water - glycerine (from the drugstore) - unflavored gelatin (from grocery store) - rubbing alcohol - measuring cup - spoons - perfume or cologne - help and permission from your family - microwave oven - egg beater

WHAT TO DO: Sprinkle 1 envelope gelatin onto 1 cup of water in a measuring cup. Nuke the cup in the microwave for 2 minutes. Stir it up. If you don't use a microwave, heat the 1 cup of water to nearly boiling and then stir in the gelatin. Stir in 1 cup cold water.

MORE STUFF TO DO: Let the mix cool until it's just warm. Add 4 tablespoons of glycerine and several dashes of your favorite cologne or perfume. Add 1 tablespoon rubbing alcohol. Put it in the fridge.

Every 15 minutes, stir it up. This will help cool it evenly. In an hour or so, your lotion will gel like loose Jell-O. Take it out of the fridge and whip it up with an eggbeater or a fork. This stirs air into the lotion. Wait about 30 minutes. If your lotion is getting too thick to pour, whip in a little water. Keep adding water till it gets thin enough to pour.

EVEN MORE: Pour the lotion in bottles and use it whenever you like. Since you made it yourself, the lotion makes a dazzling gift. Have fun thinking up a name for your lotion and make labels!

If you enjoyed this, go to the library to get more information about chemistry and/or cosmetics. Several books in the reference section of many libraries give you chemical formulas on how to make everything from car wax to insect repellent. Ask your librarian.

The Truth about Skin

All skin cosmetics work in just the very top layer of your skin. This layer is made of dead skin cells.

Top layer

No matter what ingredients are in cosmetics, they cannot change the fact that the top of our skin is dead.

Sometimes the people who sell us stuff will say that a new secret or an old-fashioned herb or some fruit or vegetable juice will penetrate skin and make it softer and younger.

It's just advertising, folks. Don't pay too much attention to it. The top of our skin is dead and that's that.

P.S. from Jax: People sometimes make fun of me for doing this, but I read the ingredients labels at the supermarket. If you keep reading them, sooner or later a lot of this chemistry stuff will make sense.

Dear Beakman,

When the snow melts, where does the white go?

Korby Everill
West Valley,
Utah

Dear Korby,

That question is like a poem. It's a graceful thought that the white goes someplace when snow melts. Grown-ups sometimes can't see things that beautifully. Thank you for your clarity of thought.

Speaking of clarity, snow is made from water, and water is clear but snow isn't clear – or is it?

The white you see in snow isn't really a thing. It's a happening – an event. It's sunlight bouncing off millions of flat shiny surfaces, which are the sides of a snowflake.

Beakman

Beakman Place

Beyond the Surfaces

WHAT YOU NEED: $1/2$ cup water - $1^3/4$ cups white sugar - help and permission from a grown-up

WHAT TO DO: Look at the sugar. It looks white. But it's not. Sugar is a lot like snow – clear, but it looks white. Now ask a grown-up helper to boil the water and stir in the sugar. Keep stirring. After 6 minutes' boiling, carefully pour it onto a clean plate.

WHAT IS GOING ON: After the sugar cools off for an hour, pop it out of the plate and hold it up to the light. It's clear, isn't it? If your sugar has a light brown tint, it just means it cooked a bit too long. It still proves a point: If you melt the sugar together into one thing, it looks clear.

The reason snow looks white is that snow has millions of tiny flat surfaces that all act like tiny mirrors, bouncing sunlight. If you melt snow into water, you're doing just about the same thing as you did with sugar in your experiment.

By the way, if you put a couple drops of orange or lemon extract into your experiment, you'll end up making a big pass-around lollipop.

⚠ CAUTION: Cooking with melted sugars is very dangerous. The temperatures get as high as 310°. It's really important to get help from grown-ups for this experiment. Have a little patience if they can't do it right now.

The Shape of Snow

Snow has 2 shapes – long columns that look like tiny little sticks and snowflakes. Snowflakes always have 6 points.

Sometimes you'll see people cut snowflakes with 8 points out of paper. Sometimes you'll see an 8-point snowflake in an ad. They're completely wrong.

Snowflakes have 6 points because they have to. The water molecules they're made out of are a lot like building blocks, and the shape they have always fits together to give you 6 points.

P.S. from Jax: Even though the North and South Poles are the coldest places on Earth, they do not get the most snow. Snowfall is greatest in California's Sierra Nevada Mountains – sometimes it's 40 feet deep!

Dear Beakman,

How does a mirror work?

Luke Slisz
Rochester,
Minnesota

Dear Luke,

A mirror works a lot like the bumpers on a pool table: like a bank shot with lightwaves, like a cueball bounces when it hits the edge of a pool table.

Mirrors bounce out light in uniform lines. For that to happen, mirrors have to be very smooth with no roughness larger than $\frac{1}{25,000}$ of an inch. Rough stuff scatters light in all different directions.

Beakman
Beakman Place

Walls & Mirrors

How a Wall Works:

Even though a wall looks smooth, up close it's very rough. That means light won't bounce off in straight lines. The light scatters in different directions.

How a Mirror Works:

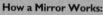

Glass

Light comes into the mirror, goes through the glass and is bounced off a thin layer of aluminum or silver. The light isn't scattered. The angle that light enters a flat mirror (angle A) always equals the angle it bounces out at (angle B).

If this angle stuff is confusing, just think of a rearview mirror. The image you see is light bouncing out of the mirror at the opposite angle it entered from. It's also how a periscope works, and *You Can* build one of these.

P.S. from Jax:
The glass in a mirror is not as important as the metal coating, which really reflects the light. The glass just supports and protects the silver or aluminum.

Up Periscope!

WHAT YOU NEED: Shoe box -
2 pocket mirrors - tape - scissors

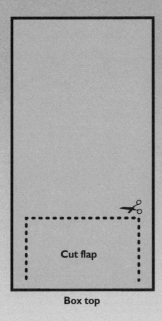

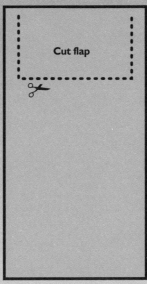

Cut flap

Cut flap

Box top

Box bottom

WHAT TO DO: Look at the diagram and copy it with your box. *You Can* use your periscope to spy on people or to look around corners. Look in one flap to see out of the other. Light bounces off the top mirror and sends it to the second mirror, which bounces the light into your eyes.

Use tape to hold the flaps at a 45° angle. It may take a while.

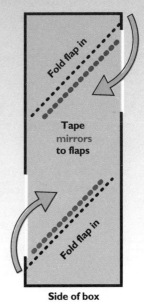

Fold flap in

Tape mirrors to flaps

Fold flap in

Side of box

Dear Jax,

Why are photos in the newspaper all made of little dots?

Justin Camaratto
Huntington,
California

Dear Justin,

Pictures are kind of a problem in printing. Photos are not just black. There are many shades of gray in most black-and-white pictures.

The problem is that newspapers are printed with black ink - one color of black.

Even if the paper has color printing, it still has only one shade of black and no shades of gray at all.

So how do you print grays without different gray inks? The answer is those little dots you asked about. They are called a halftone screen.

Jax Place

Jax Place

See the Dots

WHAT YOU NEED: Clear tape - water - bobby pin

WHAT TO DO: Cover this photograph with the tape. Press it down tight and make sure it's completely covered.

Dip the folded end of the bobby pin into the water and touch it to Andy's eye - right in the middle of the picture. Leave just one drop of water. Look closely into the water drop. It becomes a magnifier.

WHAT IS GOING ON: The picture seems to have lots of grays in it, like Andy's hair and his face. But really, it's all made of little dots of pure black. Our minds can't read the dots as separate things because the dots are too small. Our brains add together the black dots and the white paper to get gray. It's a kind of illusion.

P.S. from Beakman: Andy's last name is Warhol. He was an artist who loved printing and mass production.

Another Look at Dots

WHAT TO DO:

Look at this picture really close up.

Now stand it up on a table and move back till it makes sense.

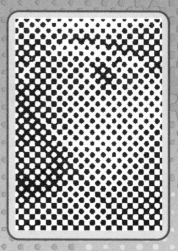

WHAT IS GOING ON: This is a close-up of the dots that make up Andy's left eye – the one in the center of the other picture. Up close, it doesn't look like much of anything. When we get far away, our minds start putting the dots together as shades of gray, and we can see an eye and his glasses.

Little Dots

The first circle is white. The last circle is black. And there are lots of shades of gray in between. The thing is, there aren't gray inks – just black. Look closely and you'll see the dots that fake the shades of gray.

When the dots are used like this, they're called a halftone screen. It's called 65 l.p.i. That means there are 65 lines per inch - or 65 dots per inch. Magazines print with smaller dots that are harder to see - at 133 l.p.i. or even smaller dots at 150 l.p.i.

Dear Jax,

Why are there all these cracking sounds in my room at night?

Tiffany Yoder
Cerro Gordo,
Illinois

Dear Tiffany,

What you're hearing is not a dream – it's not something you're making up for yourself.

The sound does not come from under your bed. Creaky creepy monsters do not live there.

That sound is real. It comes from your house or apartment and the things inside it.

The sound happens when things change size. They change size when they change temperatures. Really!

Jax Place
Jax Place

Expansion and Contraction

EXPERIMENT #1

WHAT YOU NEED: Glass soda bottle - balloon - ice cubes - bowl

WHAT TO DO: Put the balloon over the top of the bottle and let it flop over. Put the bottle in the bowl and pour the ice cubes into the bowl all around the bottle. Watch the balloon and wait for a while – like, maybe 8 minutes. What happens?

WHAT IS GOING ON: The air in the bottle and in the balloon got cold. When it got cold, it got smaller. We call that contraction (cun-TRAC-shun). The air in the bottle contracted so much that the balloon was pulled inside the bottle.

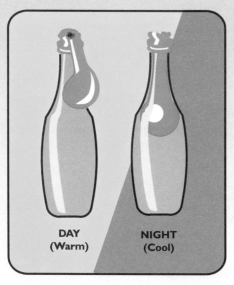

DAY (Warm) NIGHT (Cool)

If you put the bottle out in the sunshine, the air in the bottle will absorb heat energy and will get bigger. We call that expansion (x-PAN-shun). The air will expand so much that the balloon will inflate and stand up.

Warm things usually expand (get bigger). Cold things usually contract (get smaller).

P.S. from Beakman: All this popping, snapping and cracking happens in the morning, too. We don't hear it as well because we're up and busy and making our own noises in the morning.

So What

Things That Go Bump in the Night

In your experiment, air and the balloon contracted and expanded. Both are flexible, soft or stretchy. They don't make sounds when they change size.

Your house is built from things that are not stretchy, very soft or very flexible. When your house gets bigger or smaller, it will make popping and cracking sounds. This is also true for the furniture in your room.

When the sun goes down and things cool off, your house and the stuff inside it will contract – get smaller and make loud cracking or popping sounds.

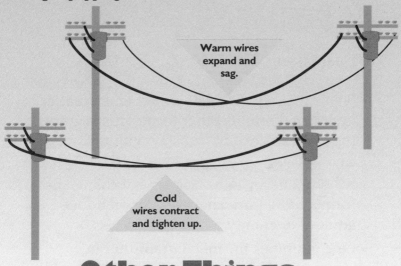

Warm wires expand and sag.

Cold wires contract and tighten up.

Other Things to Look For

When builders make roads and bridges, they make sure to put in places for expansion and contraction. The black lines in a sidewalk are expansion joints.

Something as simple as the difference between daytime and nightime temperatures is enough to crack cement, snap telephone wires, or even bend steel electrical towers if they are not built properly.

Dear Beakman,

Where does nuclear energy come from?

Jason Kelly
Concord,
California

Dear Jason,

Nuclear energy is what we get when matter is changed into its other form. This is going to sound all cosmic, but stay with me.

Matter – you know, physical stuff – is just a way for energy to be. Matter can change its form and be pure energy – a tremendous amount of energy.

One pound of the metal uranium can change form – into as much energy as we'd get from exploding 16,000,000 pounds of dynamite. Controlling that much energy safely is a very difficult problem and very controversial. That's why there's so much advertising by the people who build nuclear power plants.

Beakman

Beakman Place

Losing Your Marbles

WHAT YOU NEED: 20 marbles or pebbles - an active imagination

WHAT TO DO: Place 1 marble aside. Draw a circle in the dirt and pile the marbles or pebbles inside it all crowded together.

Engage your imagination (!) and drop the saved marble onto the pile. Imagine that the pile splits into 2 smaller piles.

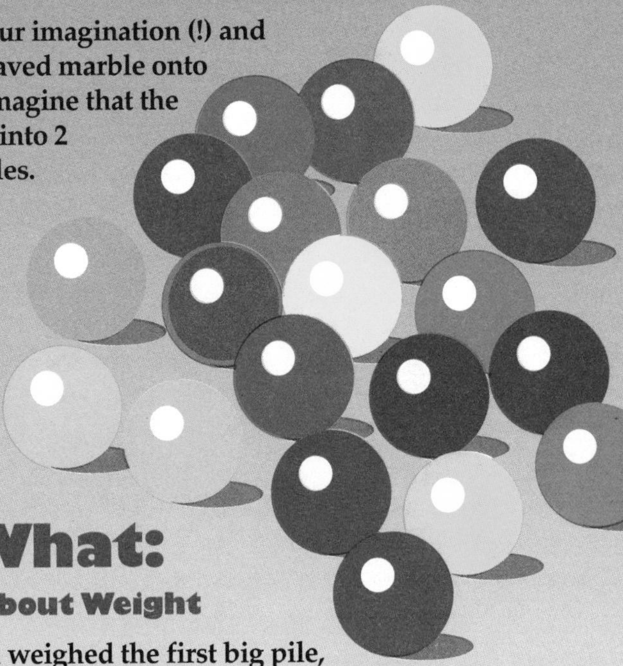

So What:

Think about Weight

If you had weighed the first big pile, it would have weighed the same as the 2 little piles. However, if your pile of marbles was an atom, it would not work that way. The weight would change.

We can split a uranium atom by firing a particle at it. But the two pieces we get weigh less than the atom we started with. That missing weight is matter that gets turned into energy. That's what *nuclear* energy is.

P.S. from Jax: On March 28, 1979, a big accident happened at the Three Mile Island nuclear power plant near Middletown, Penn. Back then it wasn't called an accident. It was called a spontaneous disassembly. It still hasn't been cleaned up.

How Atoms Split

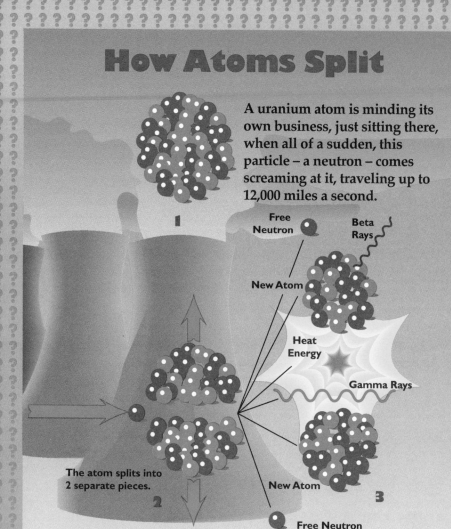

A uranium atom is minding its own business, just sitting there, when all of a sudden, this particle – a neutron – comes screaming at it, traveling up to 12,000 miles a second.

1

Free Neutron

Beta Rays

New Atom

Heat Energy

Gamma Rays

The atom splits into 2 separate pieces.

2

New Atom

3

Free Neutron (@12,000 m.p.s.)

WHAT WE GET: When uranium splits, we get 2 smaller atoms and 2 free neutrons, which zoom off to split more uranium atoms.

But all these pieces weigh less than what we started with. The missing mass changed into heat energy. That's what we use to make electricity.

We also get waves, which is the dangerous radiation we hear about. It's another thing that is difficult to control in nuclear energy.

Read more about nuclear power. Look at the library or in an encyclopedia.

Dear Jax,

How do you make paper?

Marisa Van Buskirk
Berkeley Heights,
New Jersey

Dear Marisa,

Paper is made from cellulose (SELL-u-los), which is in plant fibers. The cellulose is made by grinding up trees and dumping the pulp in acid. But recycling uses cellulose over and over again.

Recycled paper can be made with less electricity, with less water, with a lot less pollution, and it saves trees from being cut down.

Beakman first answered this question 2 years ago. It's the topic most people write in about.

Jax Place
Jax Place

Recycled Paper Procedure

Follow this step-by-step.

First, some information:

⚠ Making recycled paper is messy. It is also a lot of fun. Someone will have to use a food processor and an electric iron. Both can be dangerous. So make sure that you get help on this project because it is a big one. It is best to do this with some friends and family. That way you can spread the mess and the fun around.

WHAT YOU NEED: 2 full newspaper pages torn into 2-inch squares - food processor - 2 tablespoons white glue - 2 or 3 cups water - sink with 4 inches water - old panty hose - coat hangers - electric iron
OPTIONAL: *insect screen - strainer - food coloring - dryer lint*

Step 1

Undo the coat hanger and use the wire to make a flat square about 6 by 6 inches big. Stretch one leg of the panty hose over it. Take your time; it could snag. If you put tape on the ends of the wire, it will snag less. Make sure it is *tight and flat.* Tie knots in the hose. Use the other leg for another piece of paper. You will need one frame for every piece of paper you make. You might want to make more than one or two.

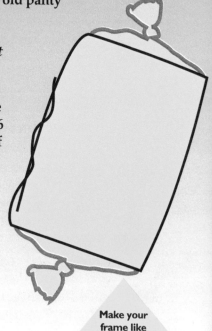

Make your frame like this.

Step 2

Put a handful of the paper and some water into the food processor. Close the food processor and turn it on high. Keep adding paper and water until you have a big gray blob. You may have to add a little more water to keep things moving smoothly. Keep the food processor on until all the paper has *disappeared*. Then leave it on for 2 whole minutes. Put the glue in the sink water and add all of the paper pulp you just made. Mix it really well. Use your hands.

Mix up the sink water again and then scoop the frame to the bottom of the sink. Lift it real slow. Count to 20 slowly while you are lifting. Let the water drain out for about a minute. Mix up the sink every time you make a new piece.

Step 3

The ink in the newspaper makes the paper pulp look like a blob of gross gray gunk.

Try other things like the screen or a strainer. Try adding *lots* of food coloring, or lint, or leaves, to the food processor.

Now you have to hang the frames on a clothesline or put them out in the sun. Wait until they are completely dry with **no dampness at all**. *You Can* then gently peel off the paper. Have a grown-up use the iron – set on the hottest setting – to steam out your paper. *You Can* keep making paper until the pulp is all strained out of the sink.

See how strong your paper is. Trim it with scissors. Write on it. It is strong. We'd love it if you sent us a letter on recycled paper you made yourself!

Dear Beakman,

What is plastic made of?

Kate Denissen
Stevens Point,
Wisconsin

Dear Kate,

The word "plastic" means *able to be molded*. What we *call* plastic is usually made out of crude oil or coal. Plastic molecules are created by chemists. They do not exist in nature.

Some plastics melt when they get hotter. They are called thermo-plastic plastics. They behave like wax – soft when hot and hard when cold.

Other plastics get harder when they get hot. They are called thermo-setting plastics. They're like an egg. When you hard-boil one, it gets harder and won't get soft again. The subject of plastics is a large one. Go to the library and look up more in an encyclopedia!

Beakman

Beakman Place

Where Does Plastic Come From?

Ethylene

Polyethylene

Like everything else, plastics are made from molecules (MOLL-e-kuuls). Molecules for plastics are very, very long and a little like snakes. That shape gives them strength and flexibility. But molecules like that don't happen in nature. We have to make them.

Ethylene (ETH-ill-EEN) is a very light molecule found in crude oil. It has 4 hydrogen atoms and 2 carbon atoms. Those atom names are how we get the word *hydrocarbon*. Chemists can take ethylene and stick the molecules end to end in a long chain. The plastic it makes is called polyethylene. *Poly* means many. So this plastic is *many ethylenes*. A long-chain molecule made by chemists is called a polymer (POL-e-mur). Polyethylene is only one kind of plastic. There are many different kinds of plastic, all of them with different molecules.

P.S. from Jax: There's no plastic in plastic surgery. The word *plastic* also means that *You Can* reshape something. That's what plastic surgery is. Doctors reshape skin, muscle and bone tissue.

The Good News Is Bad News

Plastic is waterproof, very long-lasting and cheap to make. That is the good news, but it is also bad news for the environment. Things we don't want to last a long time are made of plastics. Things like bags and foam coffee cups and tons of packaging. It isn't very smart.

Plastic is terrific for things that we want to last for a long time, like a telephone or insulation. It's lousy for things that we throw away as soon as we use them. Think about it the next time you're shopping.

Making Stuff Out of Plastic
You Already Know How!

Plastic is formed in different ways. The interesting thing about it is you've already done them. You just call it something else.

Extrusion: A way to make long things like plastic pipe. You do the same thing when you squeeze on a toothpaste tube. By the way, that tube was made by extrusion (x-TRU-shun).

Molding: A way to make lots of things like cups, toys and bottles. It's a lot like using a waffle iron.

Casting: If the mold has only 1 side, it's called *casting*. It's very much like what happens when you pour batter into a cupcake pan.

Dear Jax,

What's the difference between rock 'n' roll and music?

Steve Friendly
Cuyahoga Falls,
Ohio

Dear Steve,

Rock *is* music. All music, from old-fashioned harpsichords to hard rock music on CDs, is created from the same five elements.

It's the mixture of these five parts that gives music the full richness of a language.

Think of the different things that music can say – even music without any words at all. All music speaks. And all music is art *and* science.

Jax Place
Jax Place

Tone / Pitch

WHAT YOU NEED: Plastic drinking straws - scissors

WHAT TO DO: Press together the sides at one end of the straw. Now trim off the corners so that it looks like the drawing. Stick it into your mouth and close your lips below the trim. You know how to whistle, don't you, Steve? You just put your lips together and blow.

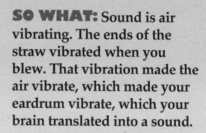

SO WHAT: Sound is air vibrating. The ends of the straw vibrated when you blew. That vibration made the air vibrate, which made your eardrum vibrate, which your brain translated into a sound.

Take a deep breath and do it again. As you blow, trim off bits of the straw. What happens each time you cut off a new piece? That is *pitch* or *tone* – different notes! Small things make higher notes; big things make low notes. Think of a small flute and a big tuba.

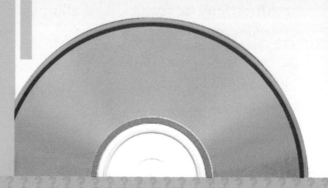

122

Five Easy Pieces

Different kinds of music make different elements more important. For instance, rap music makes rhythm very important. Even if you don't like it, rap is music, too.

All music is different groups of just these five pieces, or elements:

TONE:

Your experiment shows us about tone. It's the pitch of the note: how high or how low the musical tones happen to be.

RHYTHM:

The beat. A pattern in time that tells us when the tones will be played.

MELODY:

A whole bunch of tones strung together one after another.

HARMONY:

Playing more than one note at a time. To get harmonies that work, you have to do math.

TONE COLOR:

Sometimes called timbre. This is about the mood of the sounds. The same note played on an electric guitar has a different tone color when played on a piano.

P.S. from Beakman: When you have some quiet time with yourself, listen to as many different kinds of music as You Can. You'll hear that all kinds of music have something different to say.

Dear Beakman,

How can you grow green, seedless grapes if they don't have any seeds?

Angel Lyon
Martinez,
California

Dear Angel,

The reason a plant makes a fruit is so that seeds develop and the plant can make more plants.

Every once in a while, a variety of a plant will make a fruit that gets ripe before the seeds are done growing. That's what happens with your green grapes.

To get more plants, grape growers use a method *You Can* use at home to cultivate plants.

Beakman

Beakman Place

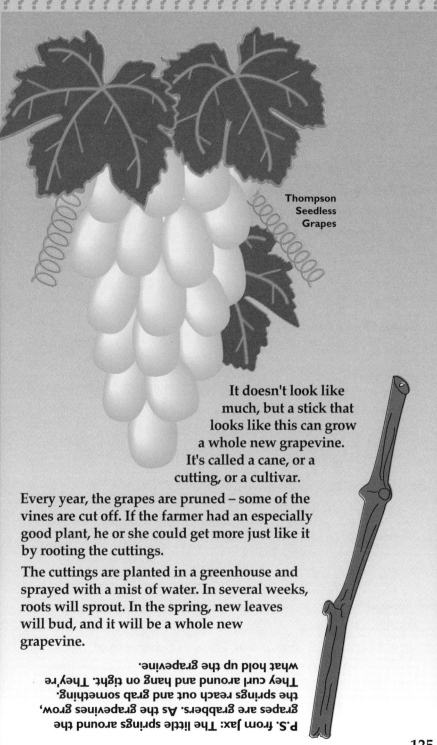

Thompson Seedless Grapes

It doesn't look like much, but a stick that looks like this can grow a whole new grapevine. It's called a cane, or a cutting, or a cultivar.

Every year, the grapes are pruned – some of the vines are cut off. If the farmer had an especially good plant, he or she could get more just like it by rooting the cuttings.

The cuttings are planted in a greenhouse and sprayed with a mist of water. In several weeks, roots will sprout. In the spring, new leaves will bud, and it will be a whole new grapevine.

P.S. from Jax: The little springs around the grapes are grabbers. As the grapevines grow, the springs reach out and grab something. They curl around and hang on tight. They're what hold up the grapevine.

125

Making New Plants without Seeds

WHAT YOU NEED: One or more of the plants in the plant list - scissors - jar - water - patience

WHAT TO DO: Snip off a small branch of the plant. Stick it in the jar and add a couple of inches of water. Now wait for a week. By then, you'll be able to see roots on your plant. Keep the water fresh, and when there is a clump of roots, plant your new plant in a pot with dirt. *You Can* keep making more plants from cuttings as long as you like.

PLANT LIST:

Tomato - a way to get more tomatoes

Mint - any kind of mint will root

Coleus - a pretty houseplant

Begonia - lots of different kinds of these

Today   Next Week

Philodendron - another popular houseplant

Geranium - a flower you may find outside

Many house plants will root like grapes do. See which ones will root and which ones will not.

Lots of plants and trees don't copy themselves well. A seed from a Golden Delicious apple will not necessarily give you a new tree with the same kind of apples. The tree can crossbreed with another apple tree.

To get new apple, pear, peach, plum and cherry trees, farmers use a method called *grafting*. They stick a bud from the tree they like into the bark of another tree. The buds will grow whole branches, and they will copy the kind of fruit the parent tree grew.

126

Dear Beakman,

Where does stuff go when it goes down the drain?

Tiffany Kehler
Green Bay,
Wisconsin

Dear Tiffany,

The stuff that goes down the drain is 99 percent pure water and only 1 percent solid waste. That means we're making an awful lot of pure water dirty – just to move a tiny bit of junk we want to get rid of.

How much? Well, the city of Los Angeles dirties 440,000,000 gallons *every day*. Feature that on a planetary scale. Yow! It's enough to scare you!

All the water we have on Earth is all we'll ever get. Sewage is water we've borrowed from the planet. We have to clean it before giving it back. If we don't, something is seriously wrong.

Beakman

Beakman Place

Make Some Sewage

WHAT YOU NEED: Used coffee grounds - oil - dinner leftovers - blender or food processor - jar with lid - help and permission from an adult

WHAT TO DO: Chop up half your leftovers into bits. ⚠️ *If you're not allowed to use a knife, ask an adult in your family to do this for you.* Purée the rest in the blender with a little oil.

This will be gross. Use a big spoon to add $1/4$ cup of chopped stuff and $1/4$ cup of puréed stuff to the jar. Then add a $1/2$ cup of used coffee grounds and fill with water.

SO WHAT: After you shake this up, let it sit *very still* for 2 hours. Look at it now. It's separated into layers: light oils on top, then heavier fats. Next comes dirty water and then several layers of heavy solids at the bottom.

Cleaning the water means we have to (1) skim off the oils and fat, (2) let the solids settle so we can separate them, and (3) filter the water until it's clear and clean. Only then should we give back the water we've borrowed. Cleaned water is put back into rivers, lakes and the oceans.

P.S. from Jax: The shapes above are water molecules – 2 hydrogen atoms and 1 oxygen atom. That's why it's called H_2O.

Clean Some Sewage

WHAT YOU NEED: Coffee filter - funnel or coffee cone - sewage from Experiment #1 - turkey baster - clean sand - jar
Optional: charcoal bits from aquarium filter

WHAT TO DO: Put the coffee filter into the funnel or cone. If you have the charcoal, add a tablespoon. Fill the filter paper all the way with clean sand. Set it in a new jar.

Use the baster to skim the oil and fats from your sewage jar. This is waste.

Now use the baster to suck up just the dirty water layer from the jar. Add this to your funnel of sand and let it drip through. It'll be a lot cleaner.

SO WHAT: You just did what most sewage treatment plants do to millions of gallons of water every day. And they filter it over and over till it's clean.

A terrific class project is to invite people from your local sewer district to visit your school. They'll bring samples of real sewage if you ask.

You Can make a fantastic funnel by cutting the bottom off a plastic soda bottle.

Dear Beakman,

Why don't spiders get caught in their own webs?

Kasey Strager
Troy, Michigan

Dear Kasey,

Most spiders leave a trail of silk as they walk. Since spiders live just about everywhere, spider silk is all over the place. *You Can* see it best in the early morning when the light is low.

Different spiders weave different-shaped webs. Some spiders don't weave any at all.

You Can collect spiderwebs and hang them on your wall as pieces of art. *You Can* also do an easy experiment to demonstrate how spiders don't stick to their own webs.

Beakman

Beakman Place

Don't Get Stuck

EXPERIMENT #1

WHAT YOU NEED: Clear tape like Scotch brand tape - cooking oil

WHAT TO DO: Cut off a piece of tape and lay it down sticky side up. Think of yourself as a bug and walk with your fingers across the tape.

Lay out another piece of tape. Dip your fingers in the cooking oil and walk across the tape again. What happened?

WHAT IS GOING ON:

Spiders can get caught in spiderwebs. You don't see it very often because they're careful with their feet.

The tiny little tips of a spider's legs are oily. That keeps them from getting trapped on the sticky silk. The same thing happened with your fingers.

Not all spiders use silken webs to trap insects. Some spiders jump and pounce. Others run after their prey and catch it.

Go Webbing

WHAT YOU NEED:

Heavy paper - water-based spray paint

WHAT TO DO: First, ask for permission and help from a grown-up. Some spiders are dangerous. Remember you are looking for webs – not spiders.

Look for webs around your yard, in corners of your house or at a park. Make sure there isn't a spider nearby.

Spray the web with the paint. Be gentle so that the spray doesn't break the web.

Now all you have to do is put the paper behind the web. Now lift the paper till the support-silk breaks. The web will stay on the paper. The paint will stick the web down and will make it visible.

Orb Web
The shape we think of first for spiderwebs.

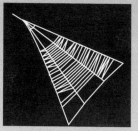

Triangle Web
You'll probably find lots that look like this.

Tangle Web
Lots of house spiders make this kind of web. The poisonous black widow spider does, too.

Sheet Web
If you live near woods, you'll see these hammock-like webs in the forest.

P. S. from Jax: Spider silk is stronger than the same weight of steel. That's not the big deal, though. Nylon is stronger than steel, too. The reason spider silk is so special is that it can stretch very far without breaking. That's the real secret of its strength.

Dear Jax,

What is the strongest part of your body?

Steve Bittner
Winnipeg,
Ontario

Dear Steve,

There are many ways to be strong: strong of body, strong in spirit, strong of mind. Your mind can be so strong that *You Can* do something no one else can do using muscular strength – tear a phone book in half.

Okay, make sure that it's an *old* one, about 1 inch thick, that no one wants. And be patient, which is another kind of strength.

Don't give up till you've learned this technique (tec-NEEK).

Jax Place
Jax Place

More than One Way to Be Strong

WHAT YOU NEED: Old phone book - a friend who didn't read this

WHAT TO DO: Ask your friends if they have the strength to rip a phone book in 2. Explain that this is not a trick. We're talking really rip it, without pre-cutting or any other gimmick.

Your friends won't think of intelligence. They'll think of muscular strength. And no one has enough of that strength to tear the book in half. You have to use your head.

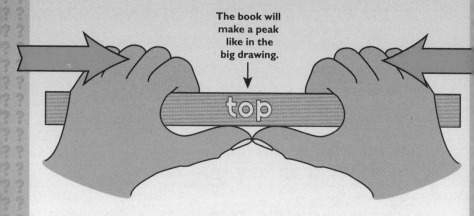

The book will make a peak like in the big drawing.

Peel back the covers. Hold the book like this. Your thumbs should be together and your fingers *as far apart as possible.* Now squeeze the book and slide your fingers together *toward the middle.*

P.S. from Beakman: If you can't use a phone book, use a Sears catalog. The Sears people decided to stop selling stuff from that big book, which makes it perfect for ripping up.

134

Get a Grip

With your index fingers pushed toward each other, squeeze the book with your thumbs and fingers. Look at the red arrows. Bend the book back the way the arrows are pointing.

If the pages are in that special peak shape, the book will tear in half. The peak shape makes it possible for all your effort to be focused on 1 page at a time – rapidly tearing 1 after another.

You'll blow everyone's mind!

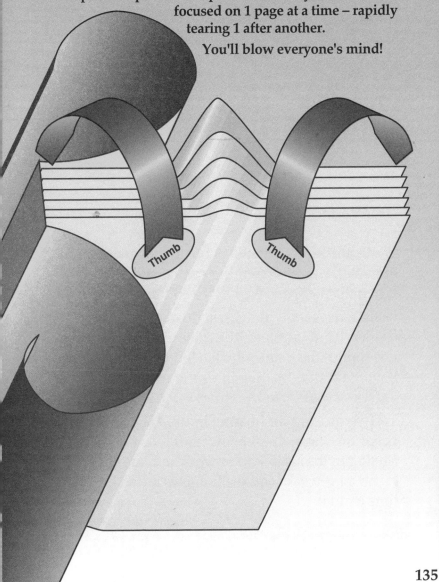

Dear Jax,

What is taffy, and what is it made from?

Hector Smith
Isanti,
Minnesota

Dear Hector,

When one kind of matter is floating in another kind of matter, we get something special and different. When that happens we call it a colloid (CAHL-loyd).

Whipped cream is air (gases) floating in cream (a liquid). Paint is a solid (the color pigment) floating in a liquid (the paint vehicle). Jell-O is a liquid (the flavored water) floating in a solid (the gelatin). Taffy is a colloid, too.

Taffy is gaseous air floating in solid sugars. The air keeps the sugars from being hard like a lollipop. Mixing in the air is a bit of work and lots of fun. It's called a *taffy pull*, and the holidays are an excellent time to do it.

Jax Place
Jax Place

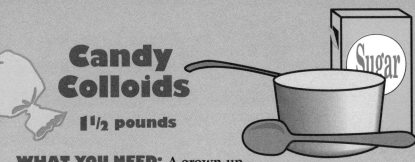

Candy Colloids

1¹/₂ pounds

WHAT YOU NEED: A grown-up - 1 cup light corn syrup - 1 teaspoon salt - 1¹/₂ cups water - 2 cups white sugar - 2 teaspoons glycerine - flavorings like mint or vanilla extracts - 2 tablespoons butter - food coloring

WHAT TO DO: ⚠ Remember, this can be dangerous! Mix everything but the butter, flavors and color in a heavy saucepan. Keep stirring till the mixture reaches 265°. That temperature is called *hard ball*. It means that a drop of the mixture dumped into a glass of water will form a hard ball. It will take about 4 minutes boiling. Remove from heat and stir in the butter.

MORE STUFF: Grease a flat baking pan. Pour the melted sugar into the pan. Pour slowly and pour away from your face and body.

Let the mixture cool for 5 to 7 minutes.

Now stir and lift the mixture with a spatula. This helps to cool it all the way through. It's also the time to add the color and flavoring. If you want different flavors and colors, use separate pans.

You must wait until it's cool enough to touch before you can pull the taffy. Be patient.

A Taffy Warning

⚠ OK, the idea here is to pull taffy – not hair. I mean you do not want to upset people in your family to the point that they want to pull out their hair. This means that *everything* in this chapter *must* be done with your family's permission *and help*. Not only can taffy get messy, but cooking sugars can be *very dangerous*. The temperatures are very high and can cause serious burns.

Pulling Taffy

I hope you have friends to help you 'cause this is going to be fun. Oil your hands and lower arms with cooking oil. Get them really greasy. This makes sure the taffy doesn't stick to you. Now grab a handful of the taffy mixture. It will be thick, and it will be hard to pull.

Ask your partner to grab ahold of your taffy and pull backward. After it stretches about 2 feet, fold it back on top of itself until you have a ball. Then stretch it all over again. Keep doing it until the taffy turns milky and isn't clear anymore. That milkiness is little bubbles of air you've mixed into the taffy. Keep pulling till your arms ache. You'll make candy and build up your biceps!

P.S. from Beakman: After you've mixed air into the taffy, roll it out into a long rope and cut it with scissors into bite-sized pieces. Wrap in waxed paper. Because you made it yourself, this makes a dazzling holiday gift. Remember to explain what a colloid is.

Dear Beakman,

Why do the wheels on cars have to be black?

Teddy Chase
Greenbrae,
California

Dear Teddy,

You are absolutely right. The wheels on cars do have to be black. The stuff that makes them black also makes them strong and last long. The wheels are called tires.

A very important part of science is sharing information. Gary Hamed is a tire scientist at the University of Akron in Ohio, and he shared his information on tires being black.

Beakman
Beakman Place

Net of Spaghetti

The molecules of rubber are very long and stringy. They are called polymers (POL-eh-mers). Imagine a plate of spaghetti. When it's cold, it sticks together. When it's hot and just cooked, it moves all around. Rubber molecules are long and stringy like spaghetti.

In 1839 Charles Goodyear dumped sulfur into rubber. It didn't get soft and mushy when it was heated. It was like tying knots in the spaghetti, making it into a net. The net of spaghetti didn't melt anymore, but it wasn't very strong.

It rubbed away like an eraser getting smaller. Scientists added carbon, and that made the rubber strong enough for tires. Carbon is a very small particle. The tiny bits of carbon attach to the holes in the net and make it strong. Carbon is black, so the rubber turns black. So do the tires.

Rubber

There are a few things that will surprise you about rubber.

The first rubber was made from a kind of juice – called sap – that comes from trees. They are called rubber trees. Pure rubber, without any other chemicals in it, is as clear as water – colorless. Scientists call it *water-white*.

Rubber was named rubber by English scientist Joseph Priestley in 1770. He named this new stuff *rubber* because little lumps of it could be used to rub off pencil marks.

The things that make rubber a great eraser make it a lousy thing to build tires out of. Your eraser gets smaller as you use it. If tires were pure rubber, they would erase themselves away and last just a few miles.

P.S. from Jax: Mr. Goodyear's invention of rubber that didn't melt was named vulcanized rubber. It was named after Vulcan, an ancient god in charge of fire. Vulcan is also the pretend planet of Mr. Spock.

Make Carbon the Same Way Tire Companies Do

EXPERIMENT #1

WHAT YOU NEED: A candle - a white china plate - help from a grown-up and permission

WHAT TO DO: ⚠Light the candle and wait a few seconds until the wax at the top of it begins to melt. Then hold the plate over the flame and gently bring it down to the tip of the flame. Move the plate gently in a circle. The flame will paint the plate with carbon.

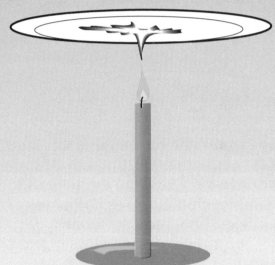

WHAT IS GOING ON: If you look closely, *You Can* see smoke at the tip of the flame. Smoke is a bunch of very, very small particles. The black particles are soot – carbon. Turn the plate over and lightly smear the carbon with your finger. These particles are so small they can fit into the holes in between rubber molecules. It makes the rubber stronger. Rubber factories used to make carbon by burning oil. This made the air very polluted and smelly.

Dear Jax,

I hate science. I'm never in a laboratory. Why do I have to know about it?

**Mark Pauly
Dublin, Ireland**

Dear Mark,

Nobody says you have to like this stuff. It's just easier to move through life when you understand how the world works. And understanding gives you power.

Science is not just in laboratories. It's everywhere. There's even lots of science in the lowliest thing in your home – the toilet. It's full of science!

You Can take a closer look and see what I mean.

Jax Place
Jax Place

Wad up a piece of paper no bigger than a marble. Drop it into the toilet near the very edge of the bowl. Flush. Watch the path the paper wad takes.

WHAT IS GOING ON:
Your toilet works with a vortex of water. The paper circled the bowl slowly and got faster and faster as it dropped *down*. That's exactly the *opposite* of how a tornado works. It sucks things *up* a vortex, fast at the bottom, powered by slowly circling winds at the top.

Get some help opening the top of the tank. Look inside. All those levers and pipes are the home's first-ever, pioneering *automatic appliance*. Flush the toilet and then lift up the long lever in the tank. Does it shut off?

WHAT IS GOING ON: The toilet flushes by dumping a tank full of water down through the bowl. It gets ready for the next time automatically. It's a process that's flush with automation.

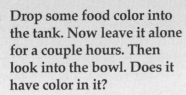

Drop some food color into the tank. Now leave it alone for a couple hours. Then look into the bowl. Does it have color in it?

WHAT IS GOING ON:
This is a test to see if your toilet's valves are leaking. If the color drips down, then your toilet is wasting hundreds of gallons of water.

143

Just a Sink that Drains Really Fast

Your toilet is designed to make sure your bathroom does not explode. Really. We'll get to that in a minute. First, let's look at how it works. When you flush the toilet, lots of water dumps down from the upper tank (A). The water rushes around inside the rim of the bowl (B) and down the front of the bowl (C). That makes a huge vortex – a whirlpool that washes away the waste in the bowl (D). The waste is pushed up and over the trap (E) and then down the sewer pipe (F).

There is always water in the trap (E). The reason it's called a *trap* is that it traps methane gas, which is explosive. Methane gas is made when waste decomposes. The water is a barrier that keeps the methane from coming back up the drain.

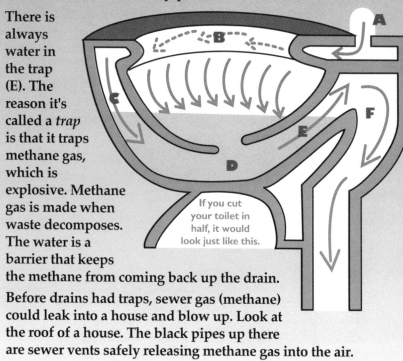

If you cut your toilet in half, it would look just like this.

Before drains had traps, sewer gas (methane) could leak into a house and blow up. Look at the roof of a house. The black pipes up there are sewer vents safely releasing methane gas into the air.

P.S. from Beakman: The float in your toilet's tank shuts off the water just by floating. That's less force than *You Can* make with your little finger. It works because of even more science. The arm of the float is a lever that increases force at the valve end enough to shut off the water.

Dear Jax,

How do teeth get cavities?

**Kaniya Miller
Chicago, Illinois**

Dear Kaniya,

If you really want to scare the daylights out of your friends this Halloween, dress up like a dentist. It's a really easy costume – wear white and carry around a drill and a pair of pliers. Yell scary things, like *"Root canal! Root canal!"* You'll terrify everyone.

Jack-o-lanterns with missing teeth and lots of candy in pillowcase bags make me think of cavities. But you don't have to get them.

Knowing where cavities come from is the first step in staying away from the dentist's drill.

Jax Place
Jax Place

145

Bending Bones

EXPERIMENT #1

WHAT YOU NEED: Egg - vinegar - glass (Optional: Chicken bone)

WHAT TO DO: Gently place an egg in the glass and cover it with vinegar. After 24 hours, pour out the vinegar and carefully examine the egg. Squeeze it.

Try it with a chicken bone. But you'll have to wait longer, like 3 or 4 days.

WHAT IS GOING ON: The minerals in egg shells and bones are similar to the minerals in teeth. Acid can dissolve these minerals. Vinegar is acid. The egg shell and bone got soft – like totally rubbery. You could even tie the bone in a knot.

Acid in your mouth comes from bacteria – very small microscopic life forms. They like Halloween candy, too. When they eat it off your teeth, they make acid that can dissolve the enamel on your teeth. That makes cavities. Brush your teeth often to get rid of the bacteria that are feasting on your leftover treats.

Tooth Talk

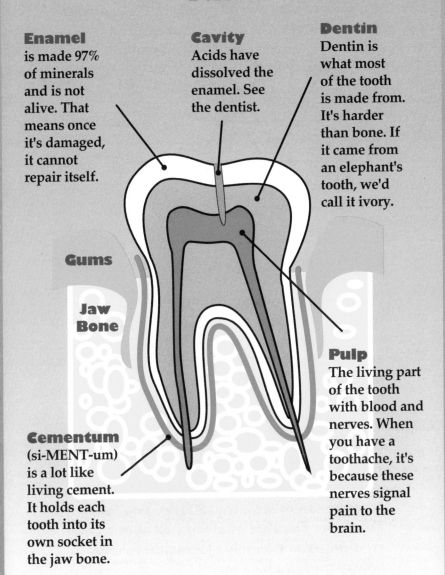

Enamel
is made 97% of minerals and is not alive. That means once it's damaged, it cannot repair itself.

Cavity
Acids have dissolved the enamel. See the dentist.

Dentin
Dentin is what most of the tooth is made from. It's harder than bone. If it came from an elephant's tooth, we'd call it ivory.

Gums

Jaw Bone

Pulp
The living part of the tooth with blood and nerves. When you have a toothache, it's because these nerves signal pain to the brain.

Cementum
(si-MENT-um) is a lot like living cement. It holds each tooth into its own socket in the jaw bone.

P.S. from Beakman: In the morning, feel your teeth with your tongue. That gross slippery slimy feeling is the bacteria growing on your teeth. Get rid of it.

Dear Jax,

Why and how do people make toys?

Tolulope
Omokaiye
Chicago, Illinois

Dear Tolulope,

People make toys so that we can use our imaginations and take a trip to worlds that we make up for ourselves. In these new worlds it's *not* just a tiny tin truck. It's a huge gravel truck in which we're hauling enormous boulders.

When we play, it's *not* just a computer game. It is the real thing, and lives are at stake! Play is fun and teaches us stuff. Play is good. It gives your imagination room to move.

Anyone can make a toy. Really. You too, Tolulope. Toys are made of just about anything *You Can* have fun with. Even a newspaper can be a toy.

Jax Place
Jax Place

Tools, Toys & Tons of Fun

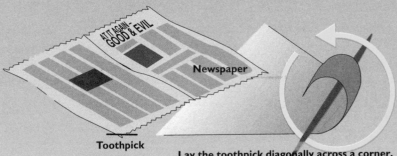

Newspaper

Toothpick

Lay the toothpick diagonally across a corner.
Then roll it up really tight.

WHAT YOU NEED: Newspaper - toothpicks - tape - scissors

WHAT TO DO: Unfold a single large piece of newspaper. Lay a toothpick across 1 corner and carefully roll up the newspaper. Do it very tightly and then tape it closed. After you've rolled up 18 of these, trim off the ends so all 18 are the same length. You might want to make more than 18. You'll need 70 or so to build a skyscraper to the ceiling.

SO WHAT: So now you've got these sticks that are about $2\frac{1}{2}$ feet long. They're pretty sturdy, too. So how about building something like a skyscraper with them? It can be tall enough to reach the ceiling in your house.

Get a hold of a roll of masking tape and pretend you're the supervisor and crew of a huge construction job in Chicago's Loop – which is what people in Chicago call their downtown.

Think Big

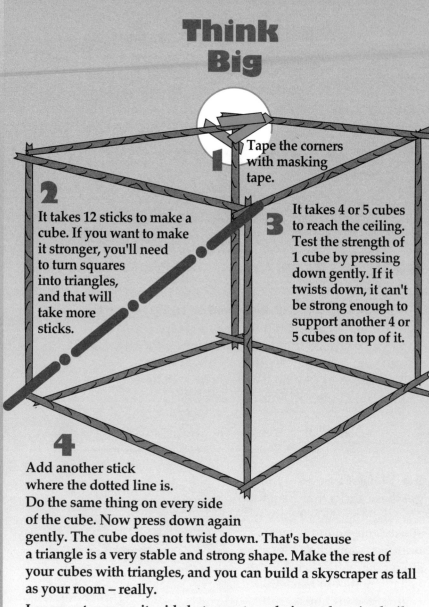

1 Tape the corners with masking tape.

2 It takes 12 sticks to make a cube. If you want to make it stronger, you'll need to turn squares into triangles, and that will take more sticks.

3 It takes 4 or 5 cubes to reach the ceiling. Test the strength of 1 cube by pressing down gently. If it twists down, it can't be strong enough to support another 4 or 5 cubes on top of it.

4 Add another stick where the dotted line is. Do the same thing on every side of the cube. Now press down again gently. The cube does not twist down. That's because a triangle is a very stable and strong shape. Make the rest of your cubes with triangles, and you can build a skyscraper as tall as your room – really.

Lay your tower on its side between two chairs and you've built a bridge! You've also made a terrific toy out of a section of the newspaper!

P.S. from Beakman: Chicago is the birthplace of the skyscraper. One of Chicago's skyscrapers is the John Hancock Center, which wears its triangles on the outside. Stable triangles is how it got to be 98 stories tall.

Dear Beakman,

Where does vomit come from?

Sarah Valdez
San Marcos,
Texas

Dear Sarah,

That's a subject lots of people are really interested in. Vomit and other colorful bodily functions pull in tons of mail to my TV show. Perhaps we can answer this rather delicate question here.

Vomit is a lot like digestion in reverse – or going backward. It's a way for the body to protect itself, and no one likes it at all.

Sometimes we throw up just because our brains are getting too many different signals and can't sort them out. That's being *nauseous* (NAW-shus), which is a very popular word in junior and senior high schools.

Beakman
Beakman Place

151

EXPERIMENT #1

Football and Throwing Up

WHAT YOU NEED: The big game on TV
- an imagination

WHAT TO DO: Fortunately for experimenters, there is always a football game on somewhere. Pay attention to the audience in the stadium. Sometimes you'll see everyone stand up and sit back down again so that it looks like a huge wave is rolling through the stadium. *You Can* give a report to your class on throwing up and have the class do the wave. It's a very important part of hurling chunks.

SO WHAT: The football stadium wave is a lot like a wave the muscles in your esophagus make. Your esophagus (ee-SOF-ag-gus) is a muscular tube from your mouth to your stomach. The muscles ripple down toward your stomach, behaving a lot like the stadium wave. This takes chewed food to your stomach. It's called a systolic (sis-TOL-ick) wave. When we get sick sometimes the wave reverses itself and brings up chewed food. No one likes it when that happens.

The Technicolor Yawn

Here's a vomit play-by-play:

1 You grind up food in your mouth. You also add saliva (spit), which starts digestion and also helps turn your food into a mushy paste. You swallow.

2 The muscles in the tube to your stomach work like a toothpaste tube. They squeeze the food paste down into your stomach.

3 Your stomach adds acid to the food paste to break it down into a disgusting mess.

4 The vomit center in your brain gets too many signals – you have the flu, are carsick, or maybe the food is bad and your body wants to get rid of it.

5 The sphincter (SFINK-tur) is like a door. It slams closed.

6 Your stomach squeezes in a kind of convulsion – major twitch.

7 The only place for the food paste to go is back up the tube to your mouth.

8 By now you feel awful. If there's time, you find a toilet nearby. That's why vomiting is sometimes called talking on the big white phone.

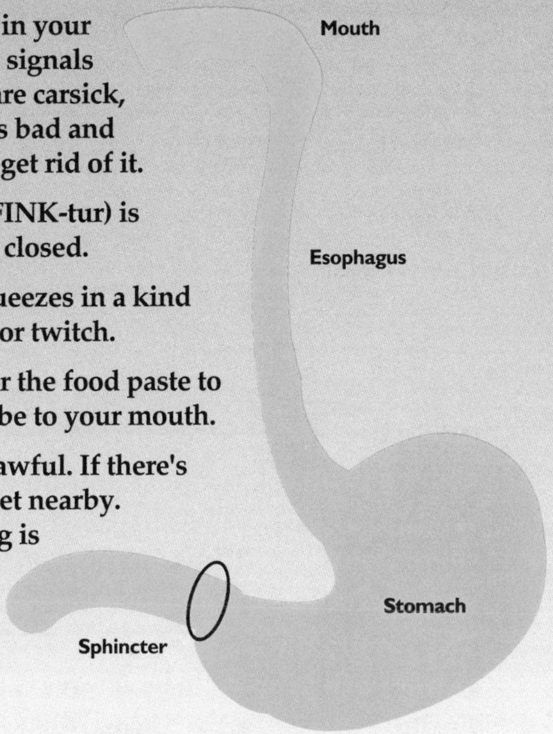

Mouth

Esophagus

Stomach

Sphincter

P.S. from Jax: You may have noticed that throwing up makes your throat burn. That's from the acid your stomach uses to dissolve food. Your stomach is protected from the acid by a coating of mucus that keeps the stomach from digesting itself.

Dear Beakman,

How does a zipper work?

Taylor Waxman
Los Angeles,
California

Dear Taylor,

A zipper zips because of the tremendous force *You Can* get by using a simple, basic tool – the wedge, or inclined plane.

You've probably seen someone using a wedge to split firewood. Or maybe you've seen a plow splitting up the earth. They work with inclined planes as well.

The inclined plane is one of 5 basic tools – along with wheels, levers, screws and pulleys. All of those allow us to use what strength we have in stronger ways.

Beakman

Beakman Place

WHAT YOU NEED: Wooden board or sheet or heavy cardboard - string - small cardboard box - small rocks

WHAT TO DO: Put one end of the board or cardboard on a step outside. Tie the string to the box so that you can lift it straight up. Lift the box to the height of the step. Keep adding rocks until you break the string. If the string won't break, start over again with lighter string, like thread. Remember how many rocks were in the box when the string broke.

MORE STUFF: Put the box at the bottom of the board and add the same number of rocks it took to break the string. Use the string to drag the box up the ramp. Try adding more rocks.

SO WHAT: *You Can* lift a lot more rocks to the same height if you drag them up a ramp – which is really an inclined plane. And it works the other way around. If you jam an inclined plane into something like a log, it will split in half. The inclined plane takes a little bit of up-and-down energy and turns it into lots and lots of sideways work.

Inside This...

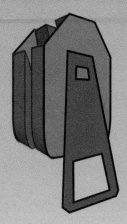

The wedge at the top of the zipper slider splits the metal teeth apart. To snap them together again, we just reverse the direction of the slider.

...Is This.

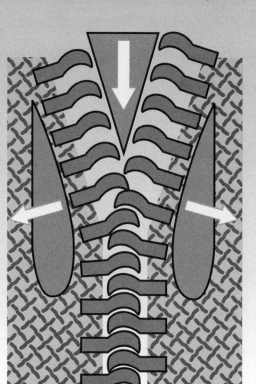

Sometimes just a closer look is all you need to figure something out. Like this zipper. Just look at it. Try thinking about it with the arrows pointing backward. The wedge in the slider takes our up-and-down motion and turns it into back-and-forth work.

P.S. from Jax: Zippers got their name from a pair of rain galoshes that B.F. Goodrich sold in 1922. They had the new invention instead of buttons and were called a pair of Rubber Zippers.